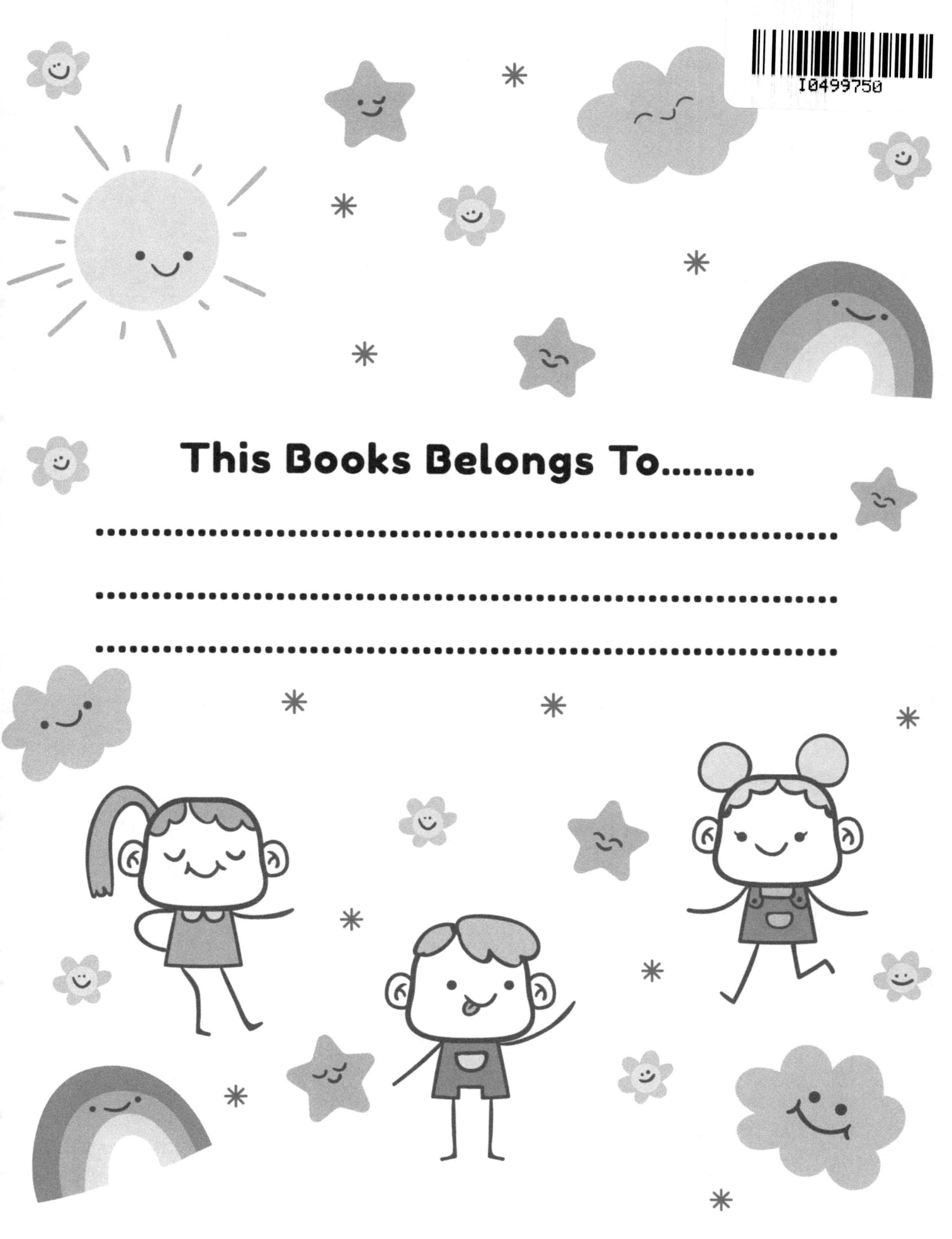

This Books Belongs To.........

....

....

....

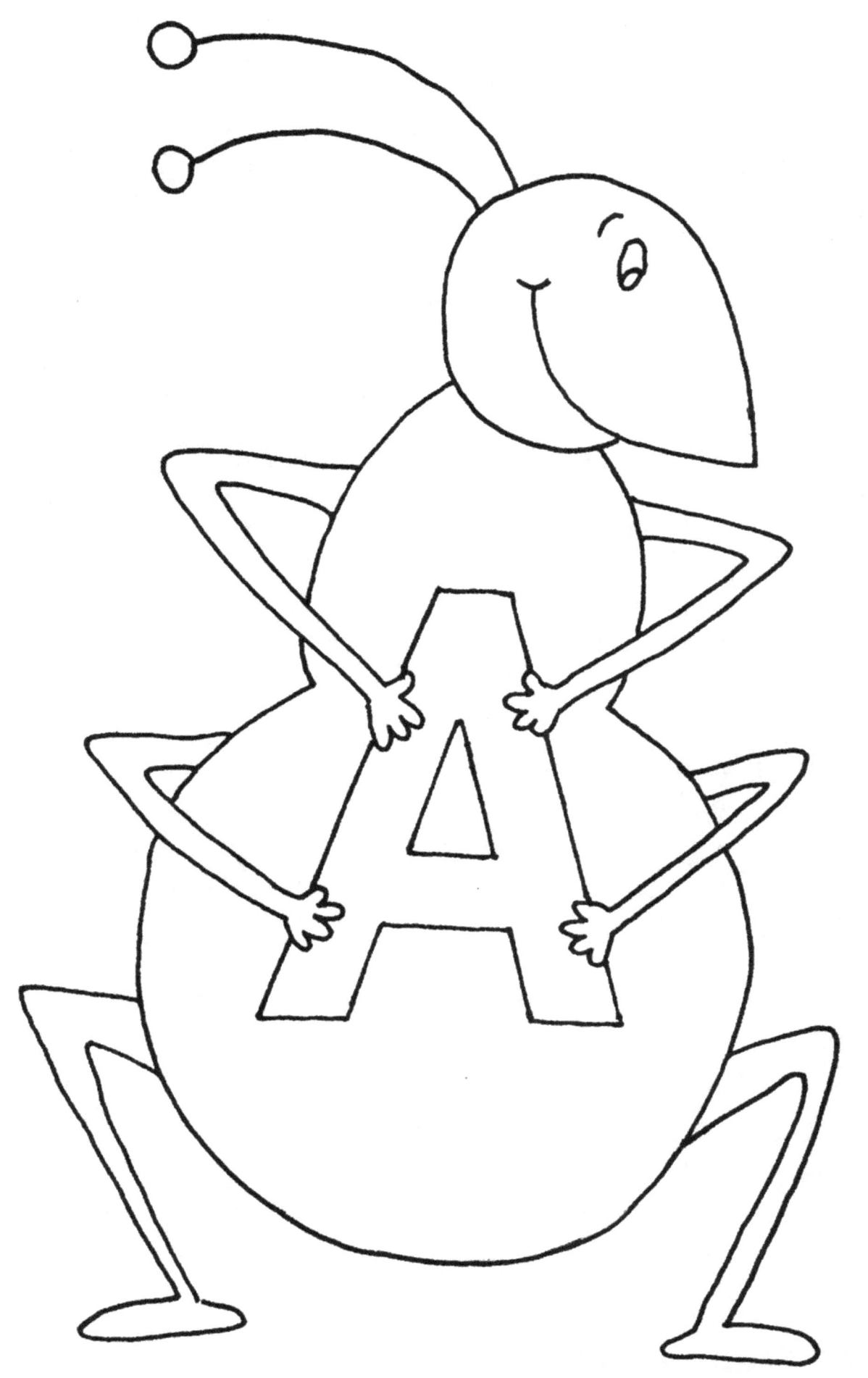

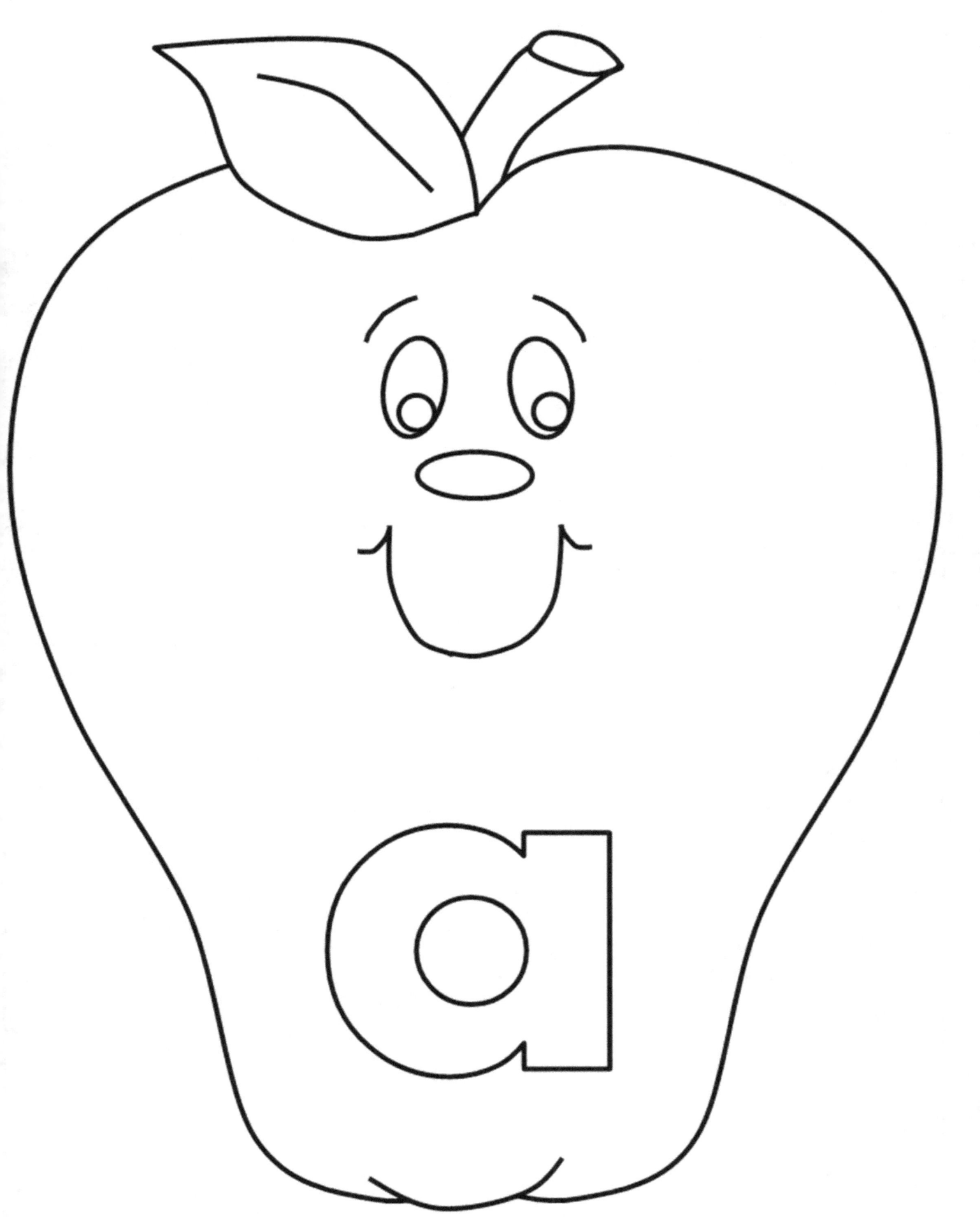

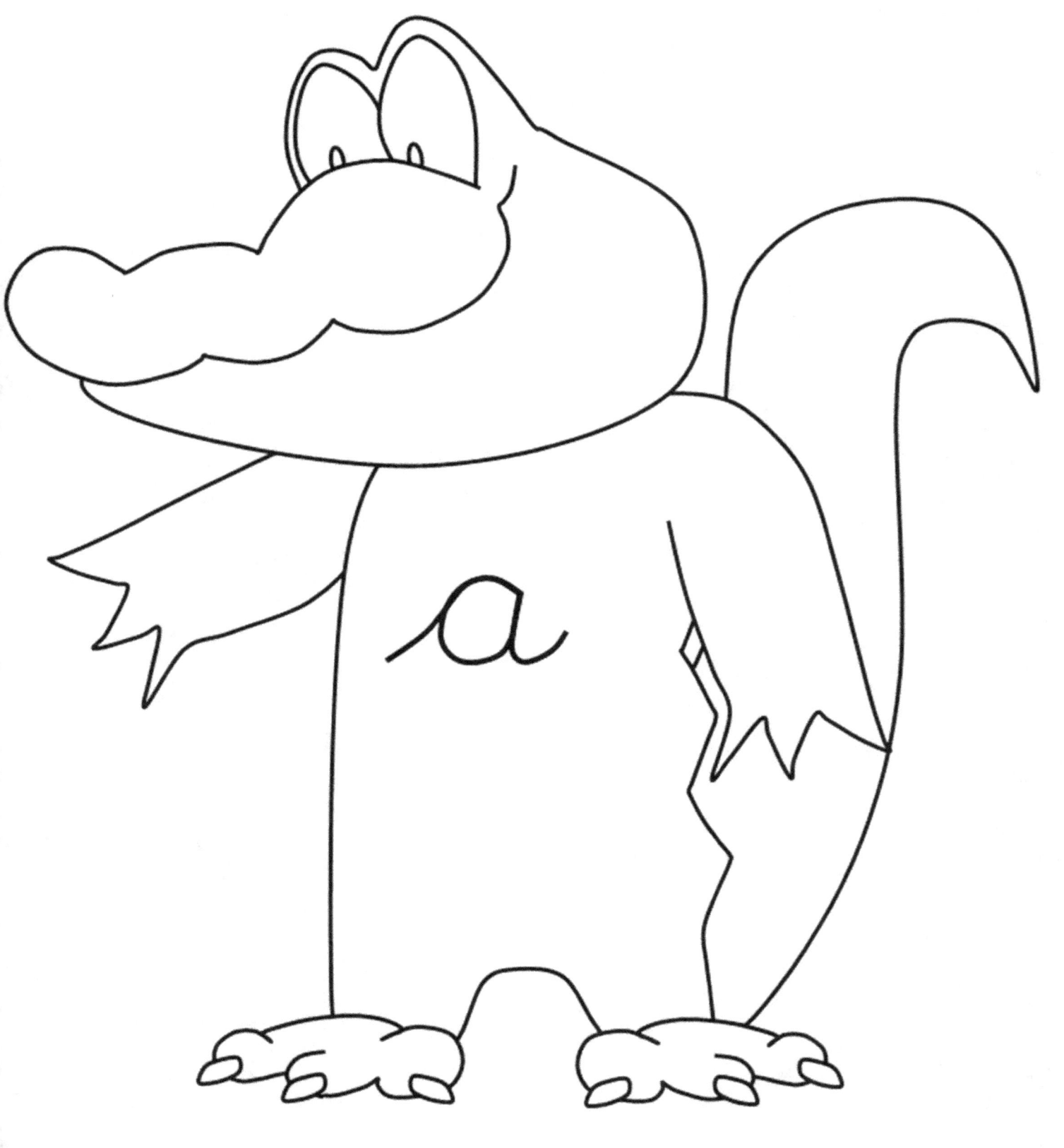

Trace the steps for making the letter a on the following line.

a a a a a aa

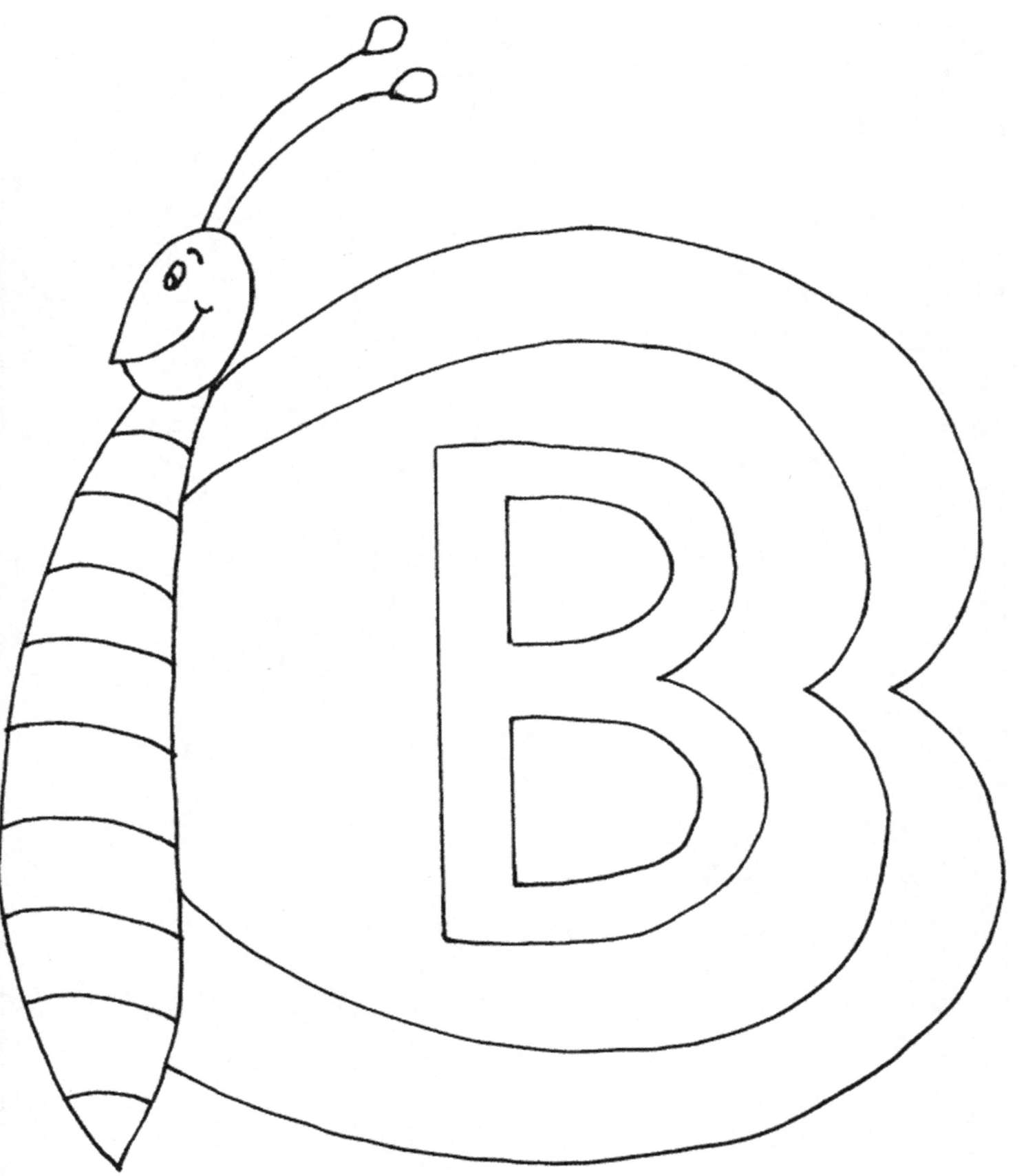

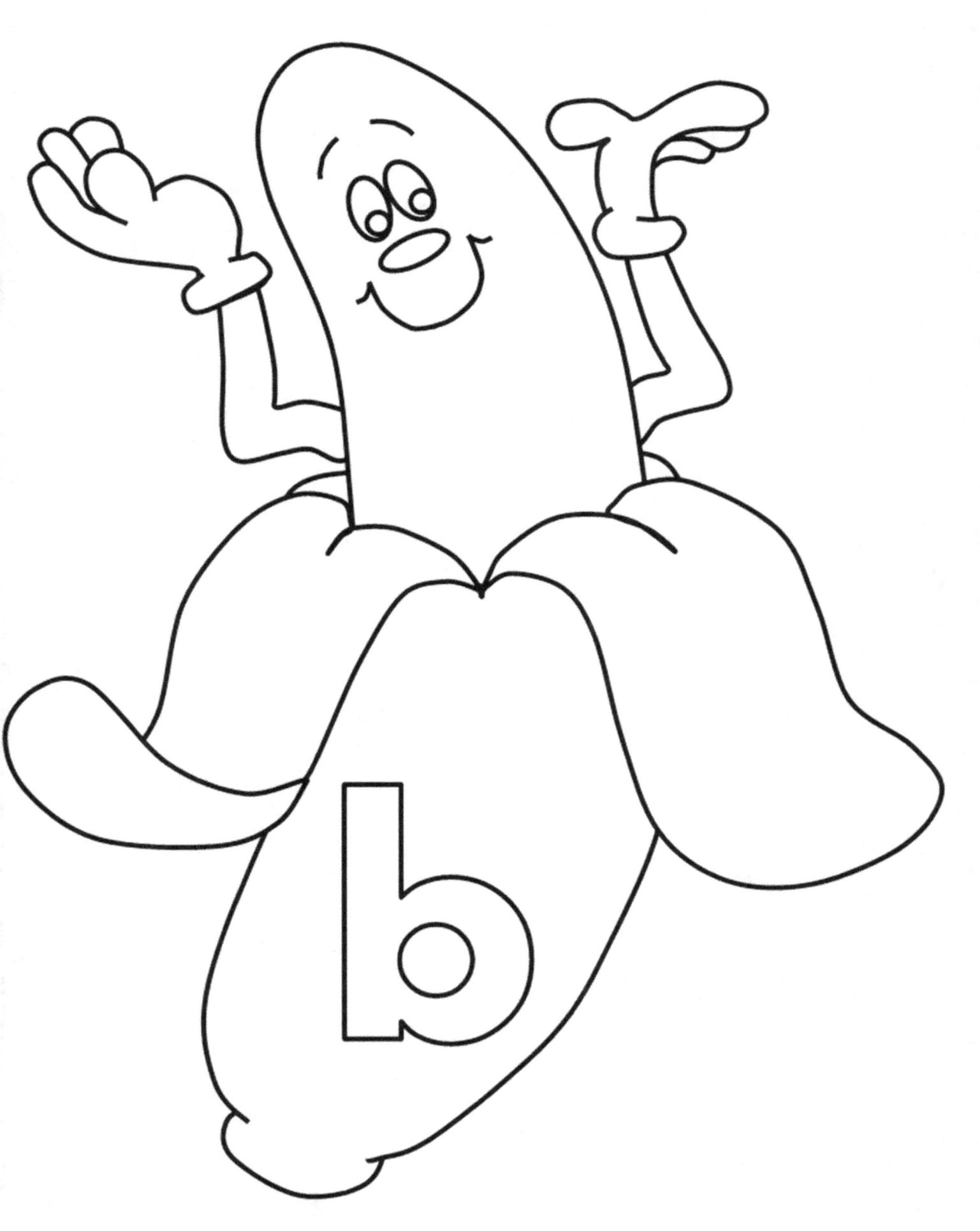

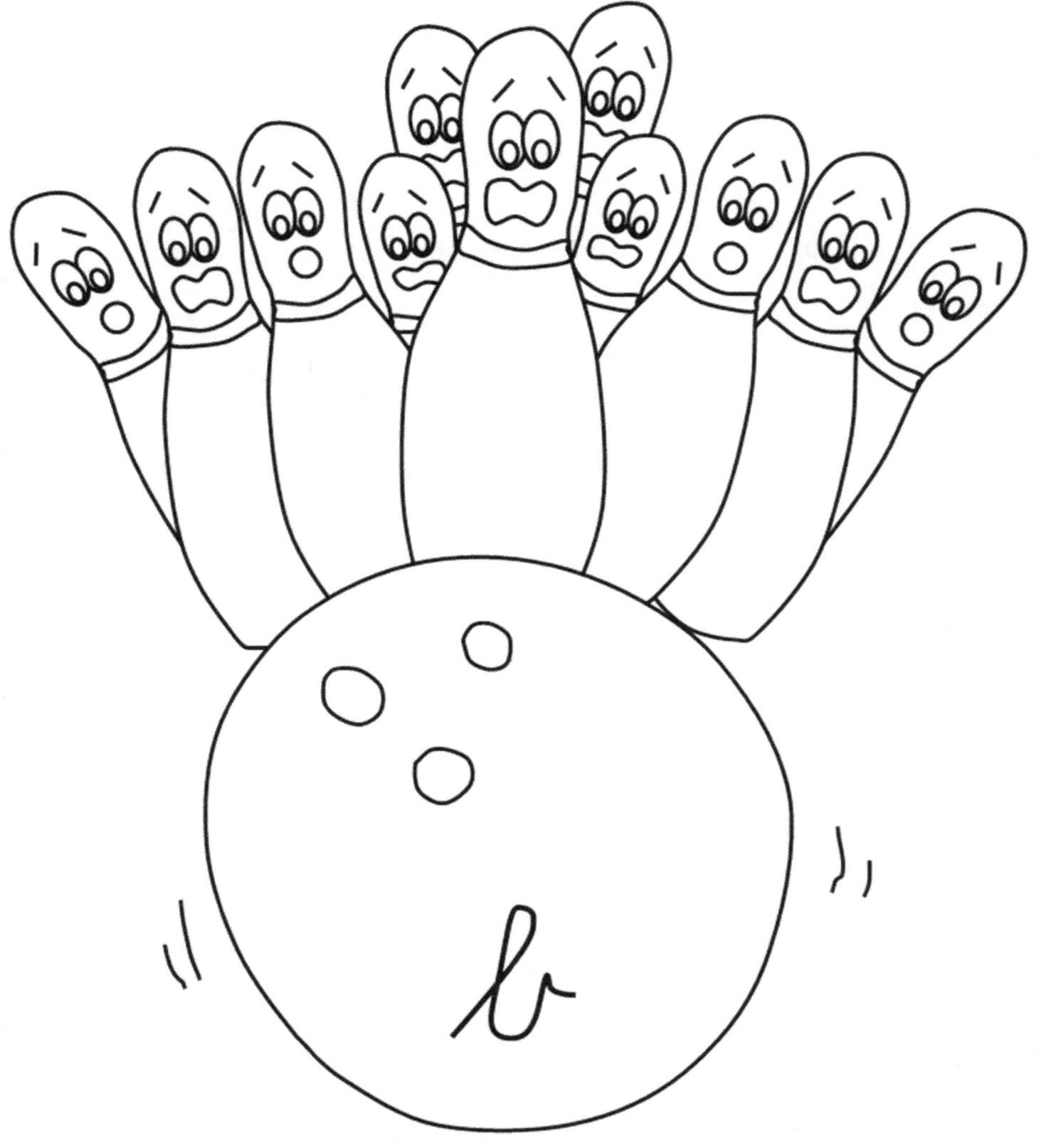

Trace the steps for making the letter b on the following line.

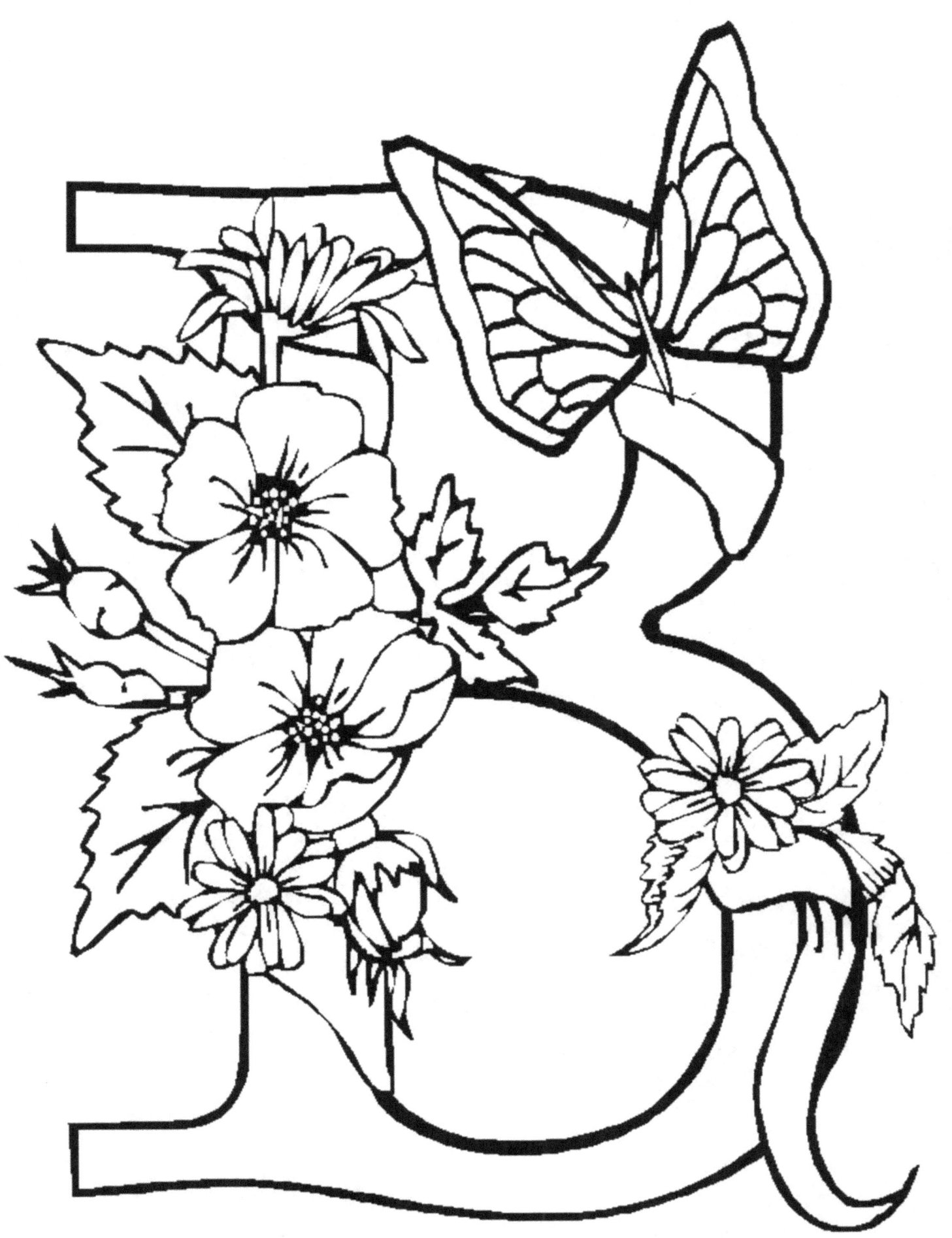

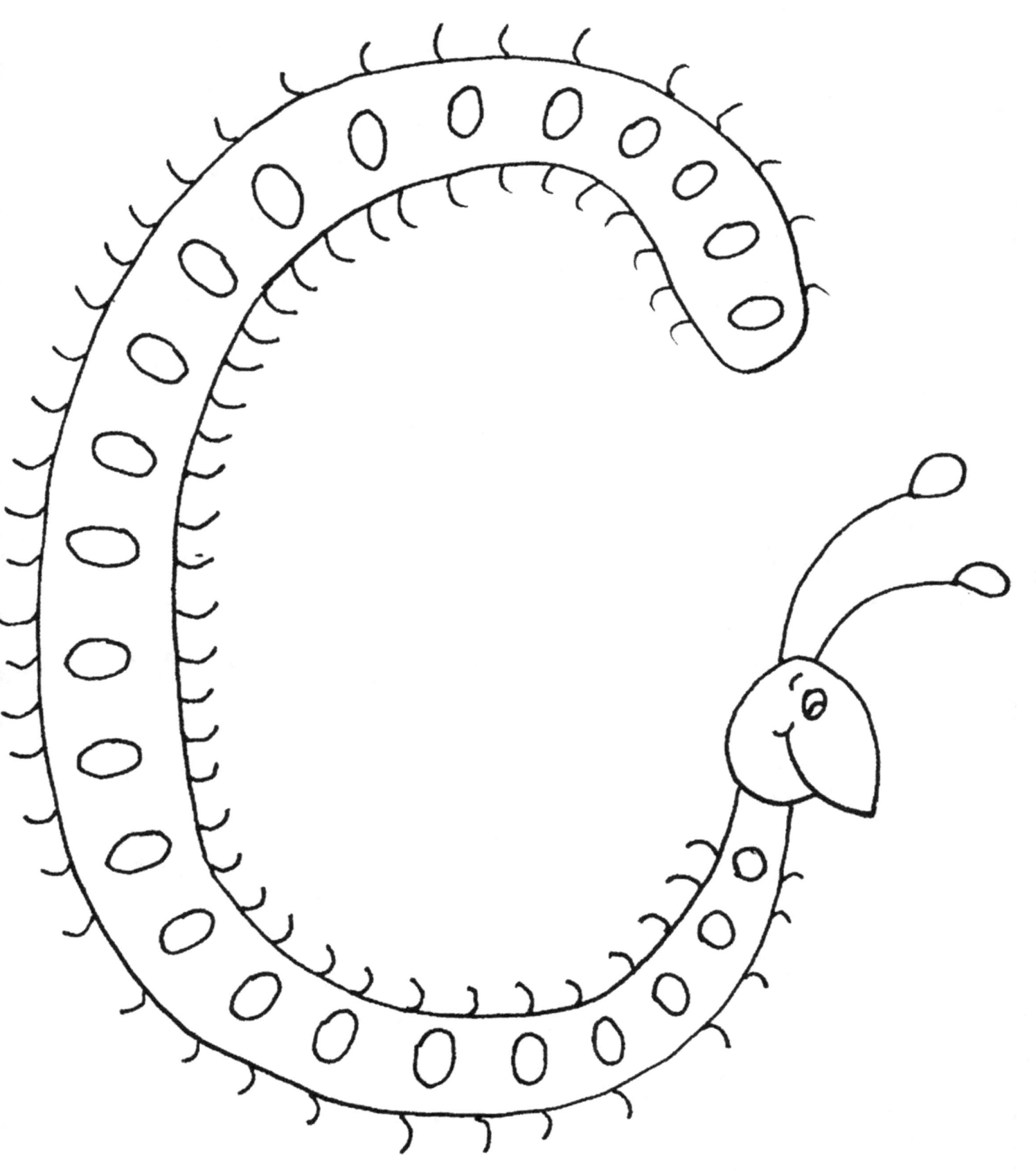

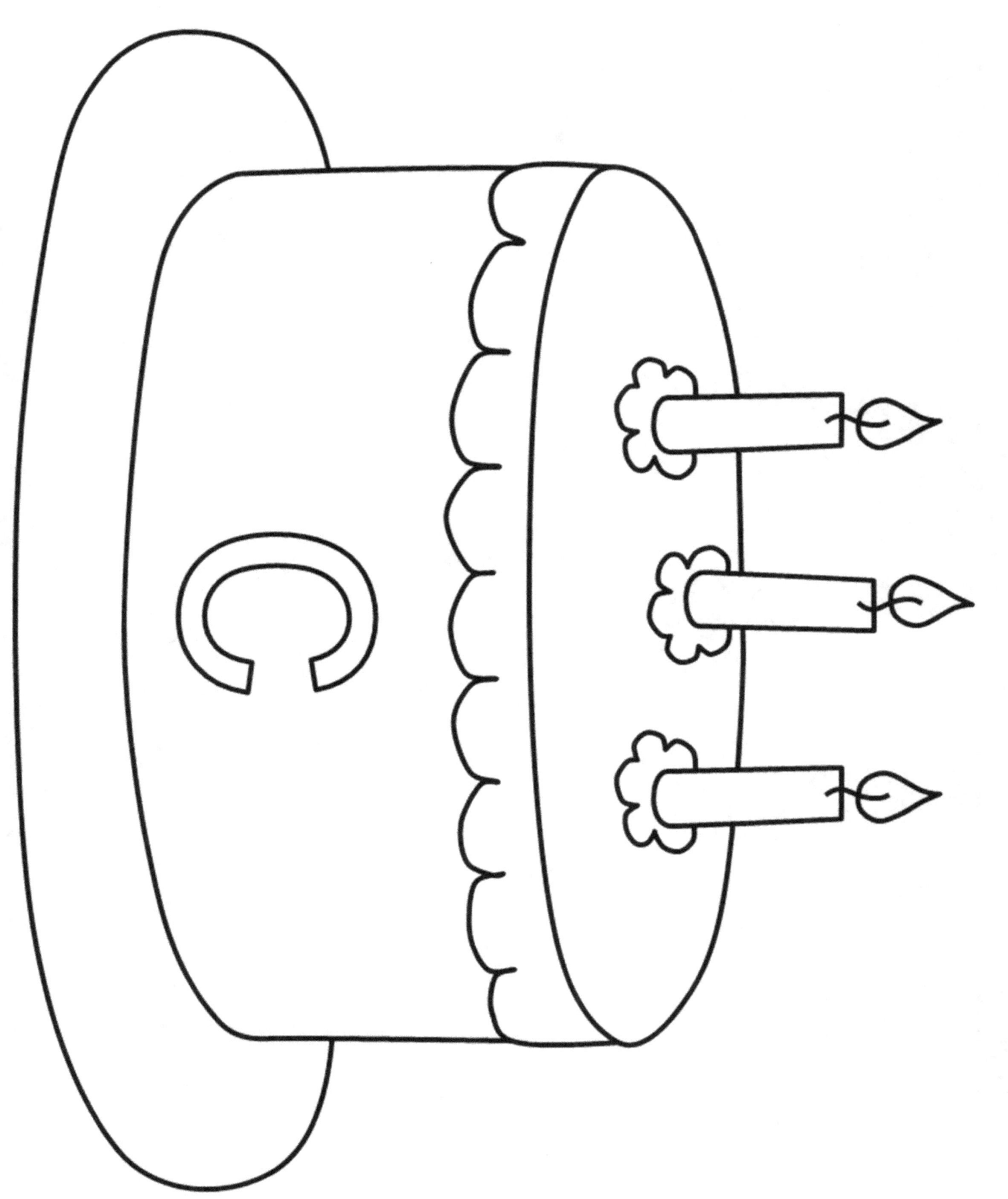

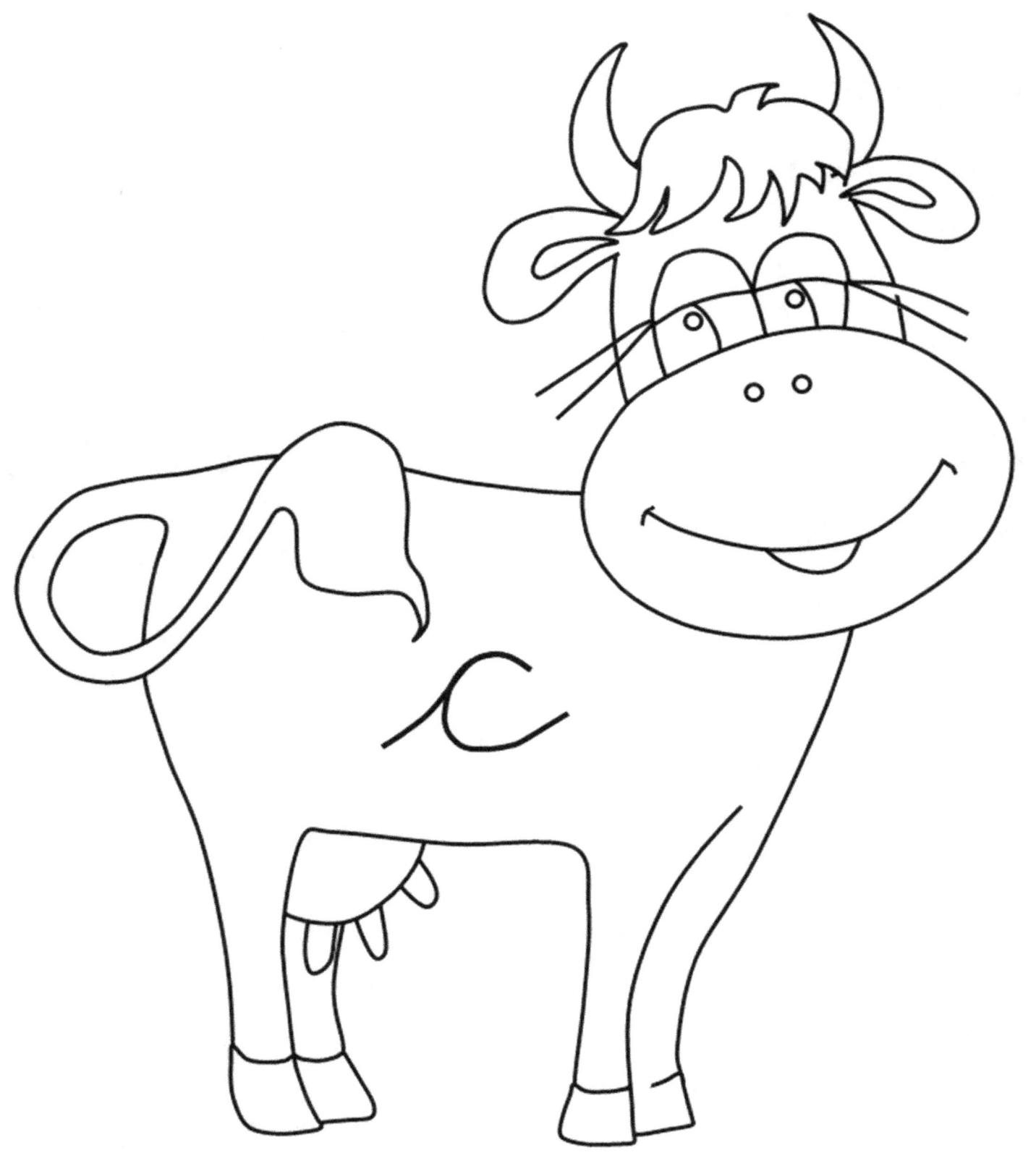

Trace the steps for making the letter c on the following line.

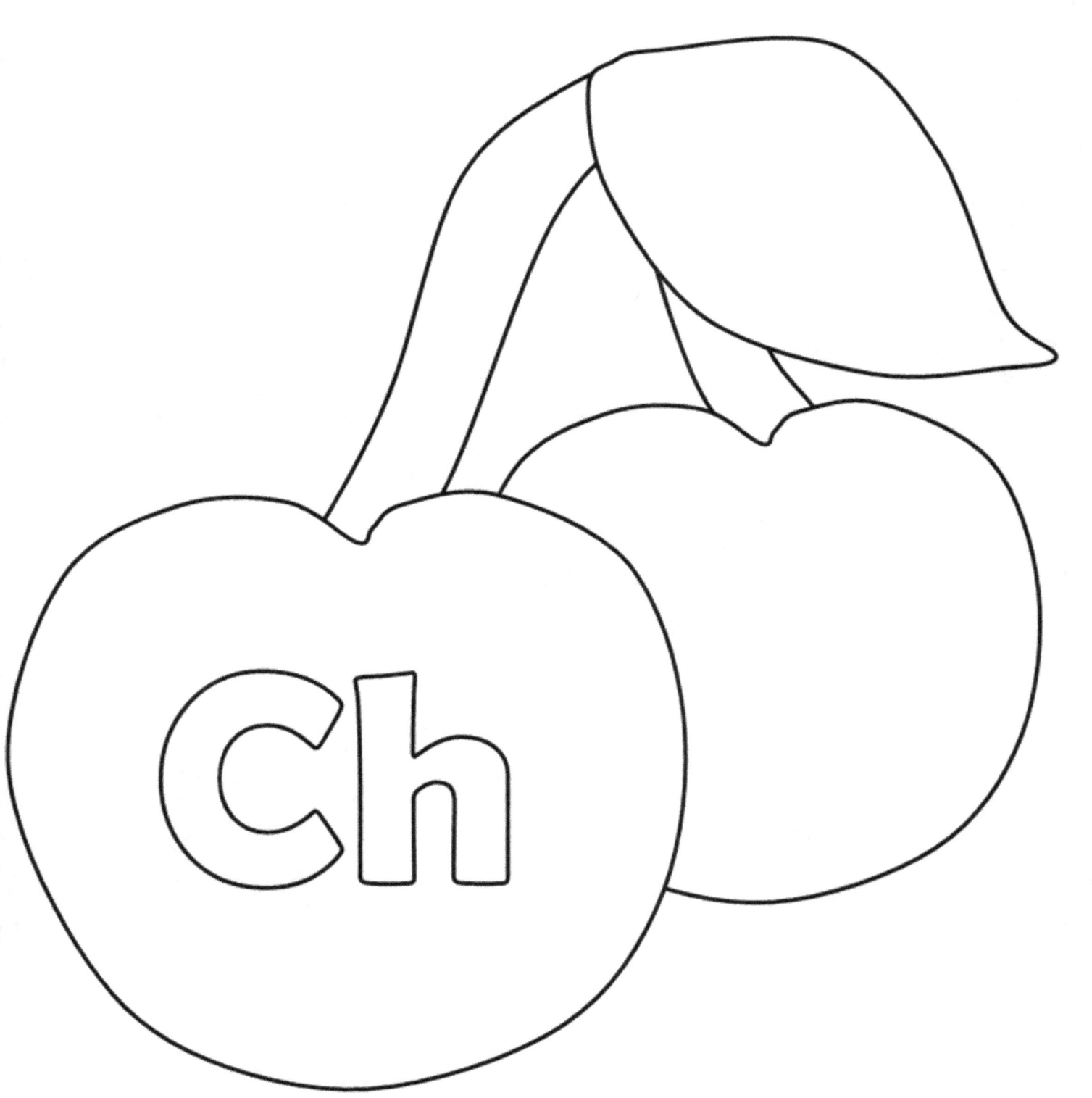

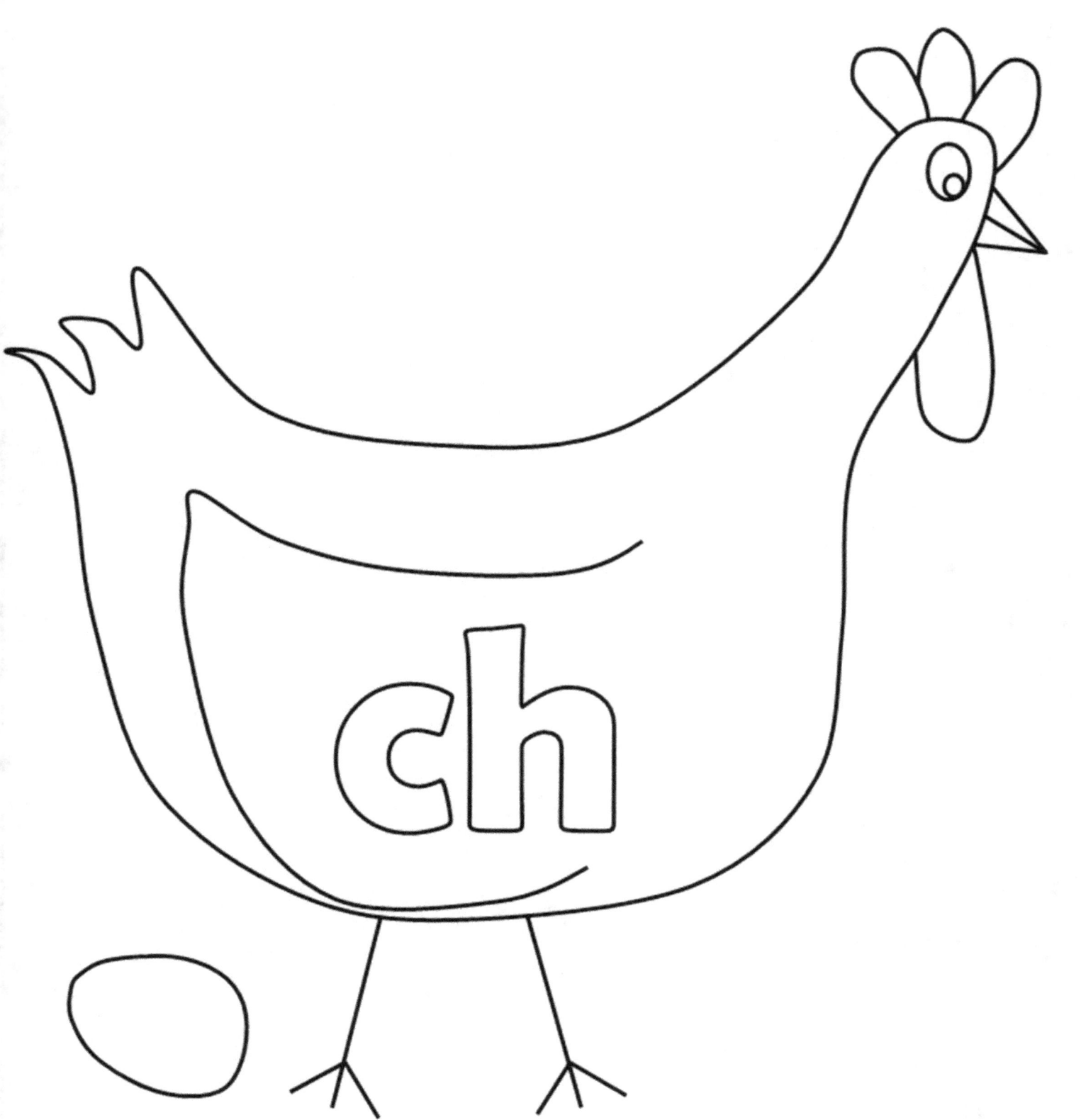

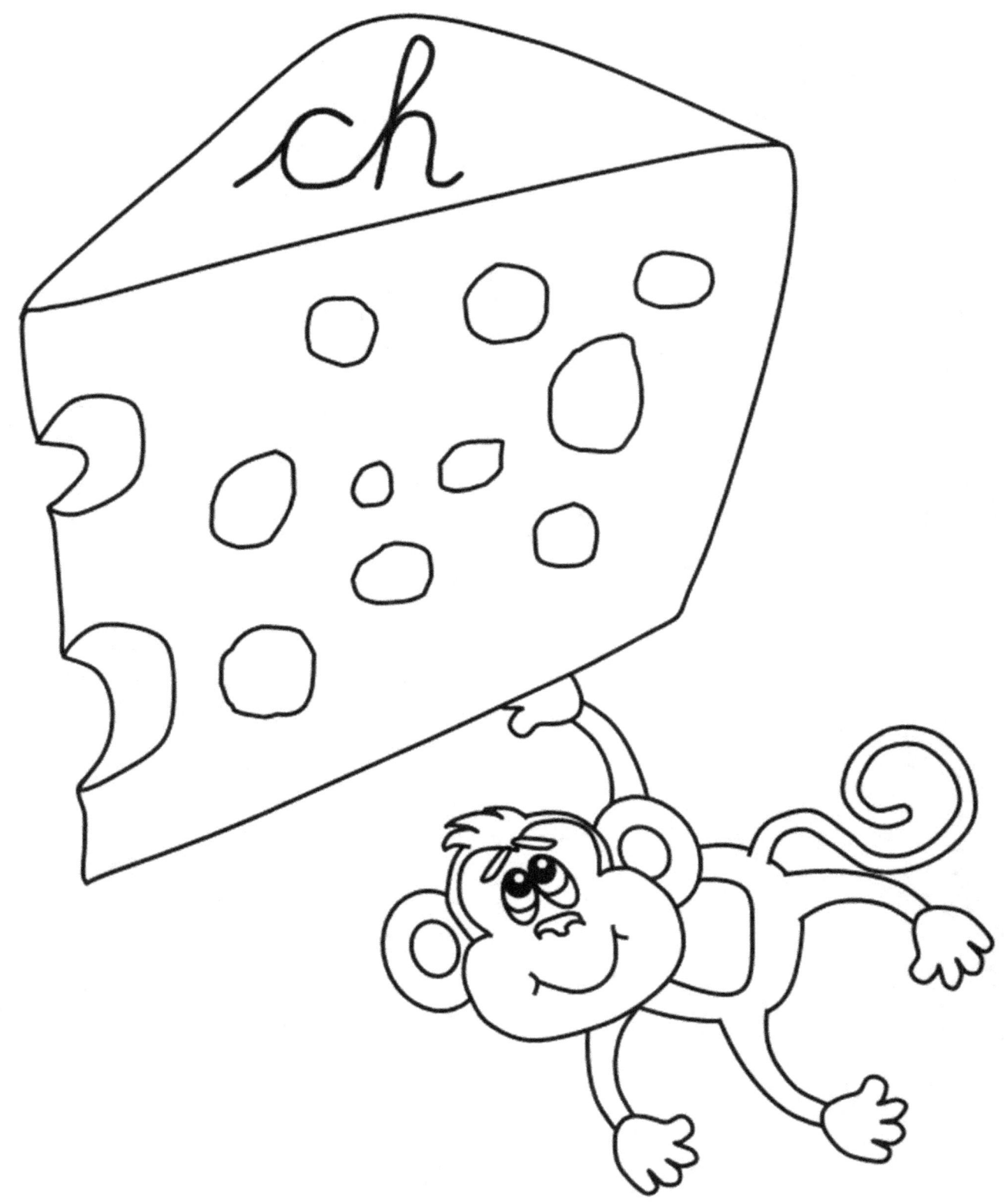

Trace the steps for making the letter c on the following line.

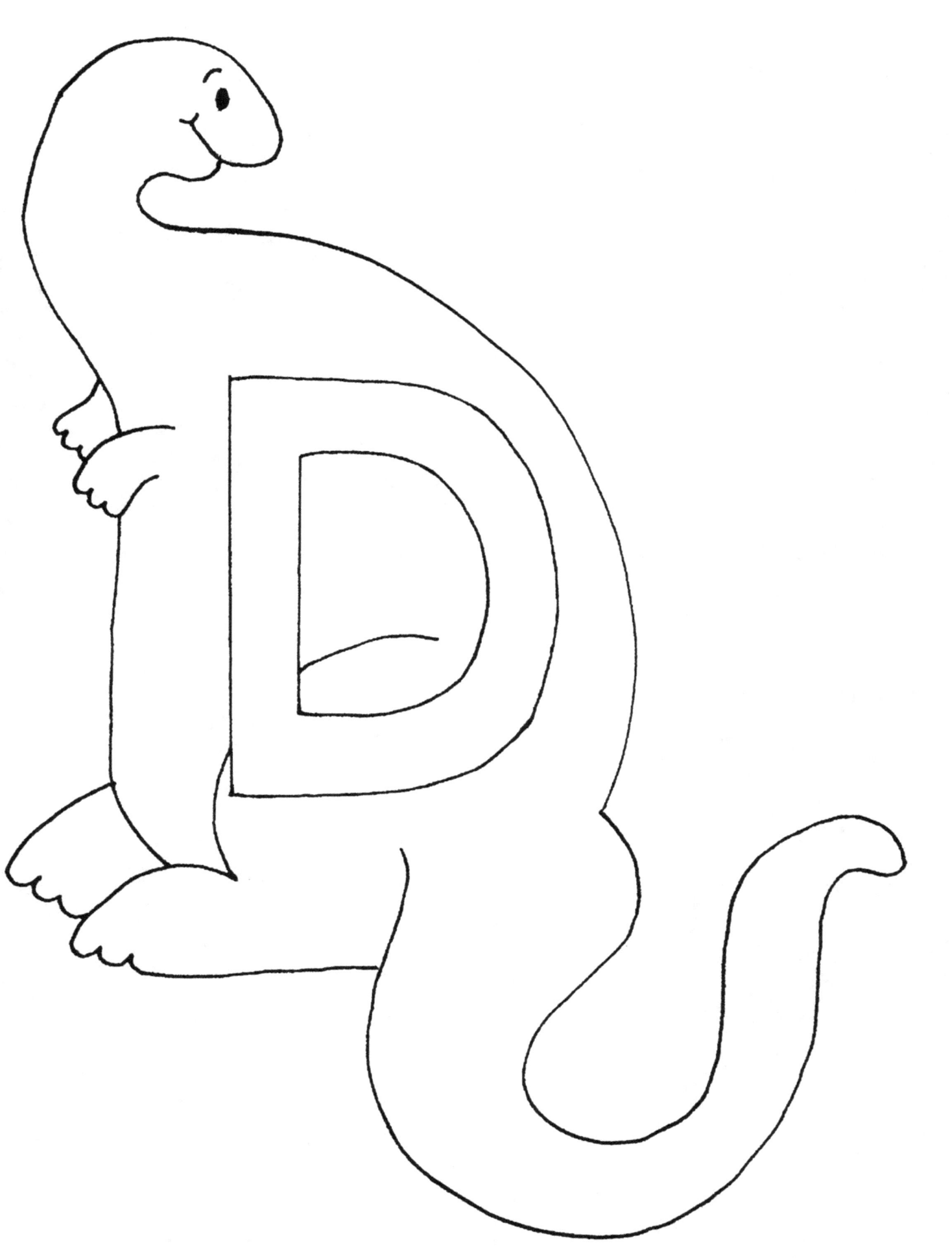

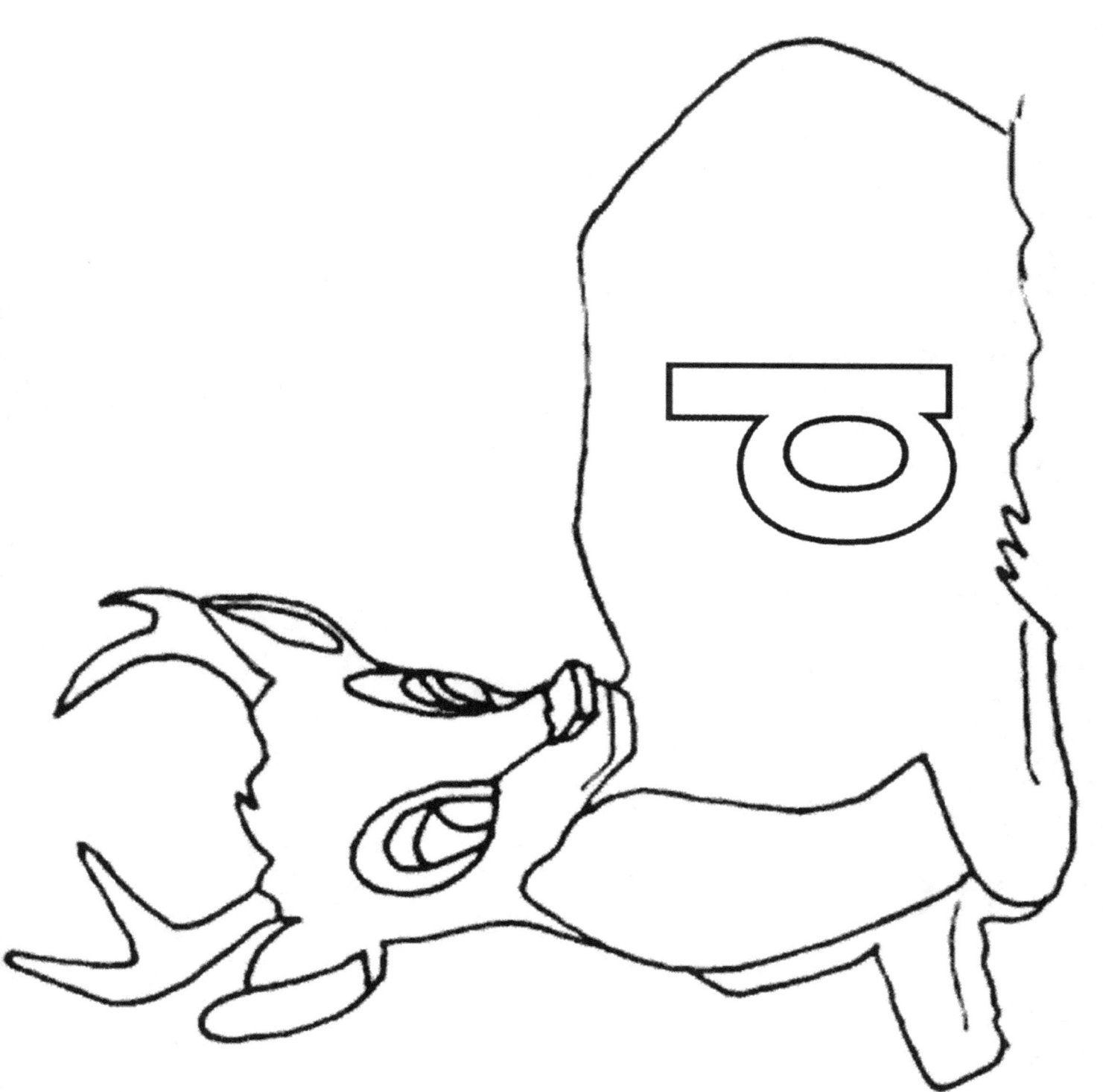

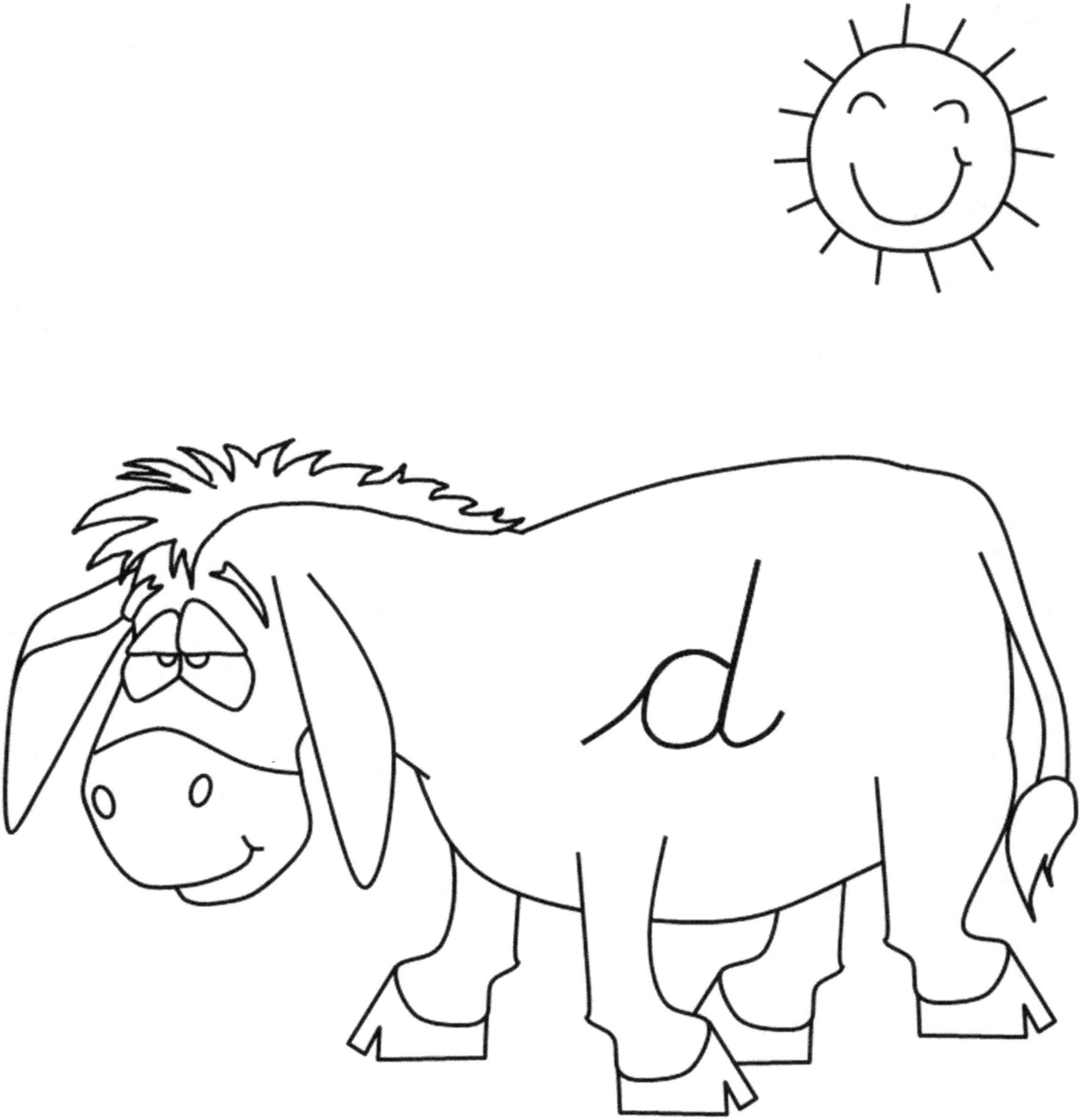

Trace the steps for making the letter d on the following line.

r r d d d d d dd

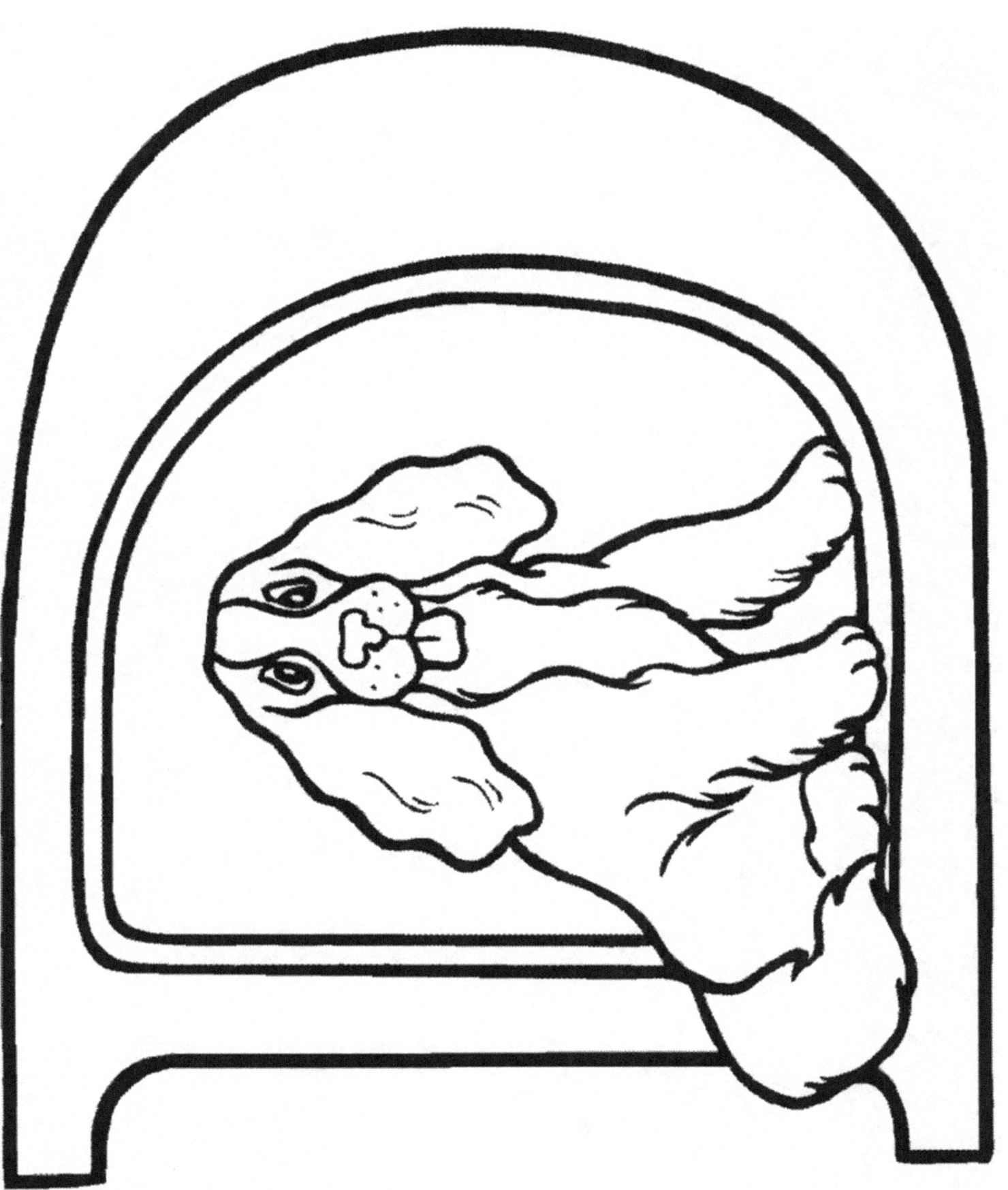

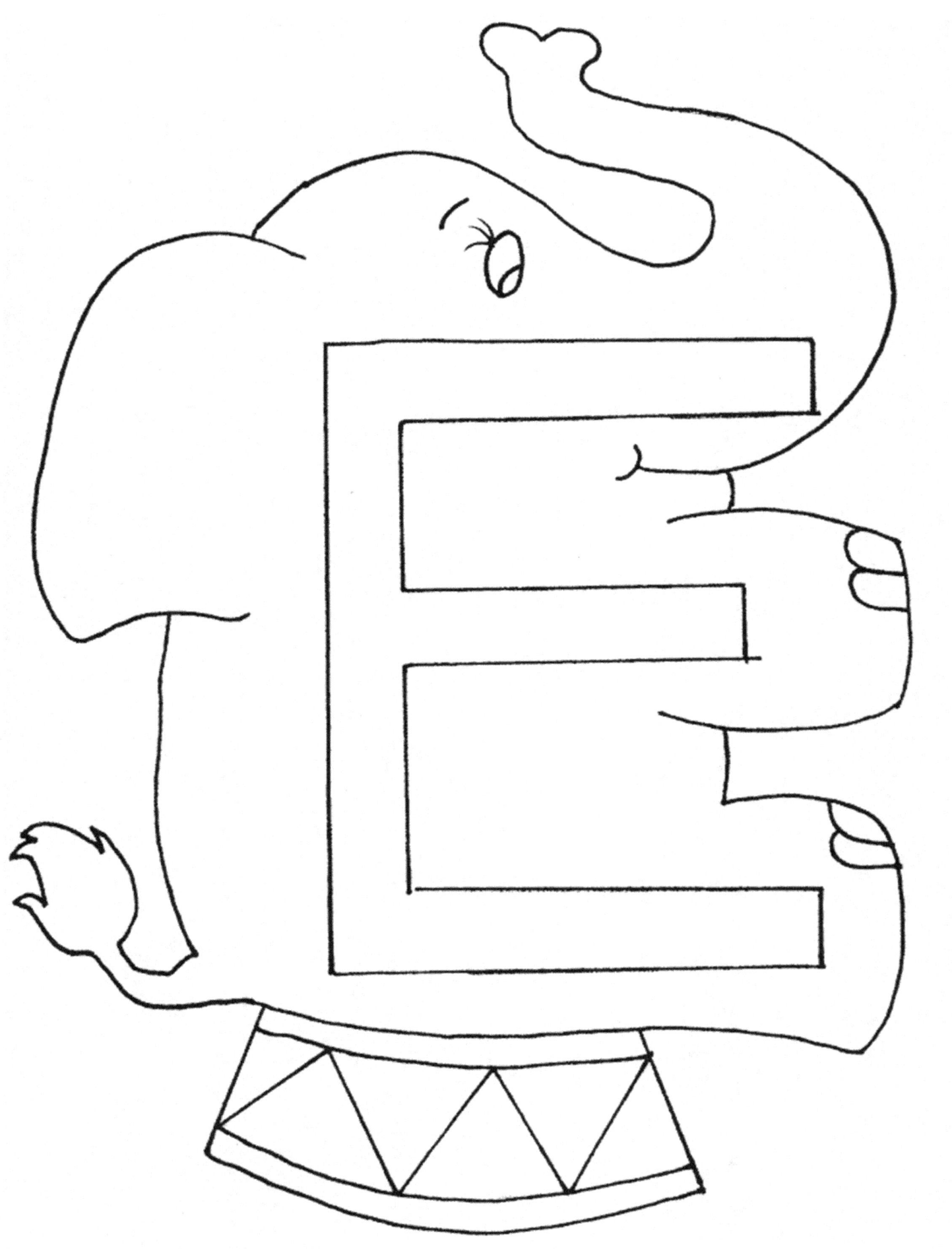

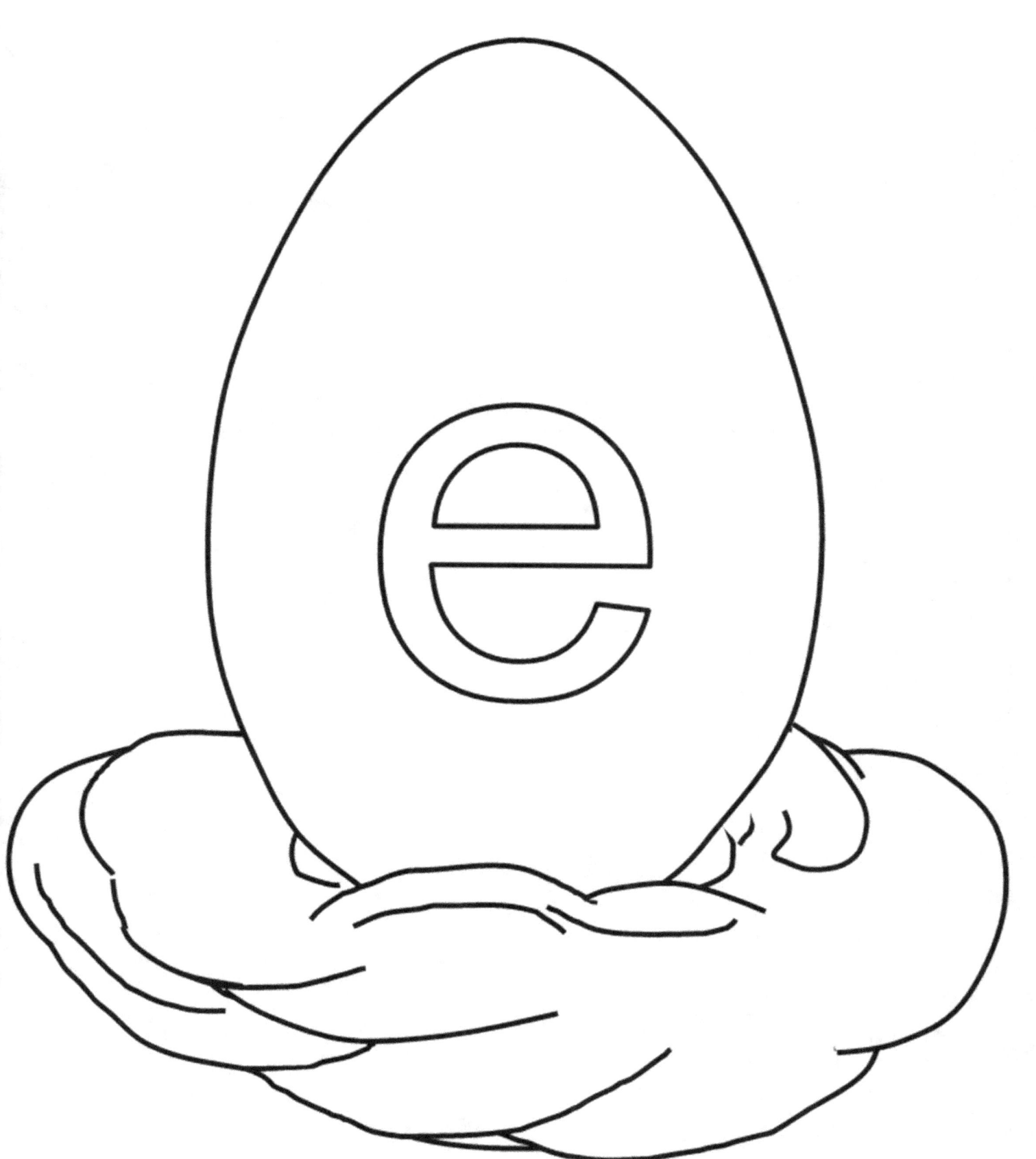

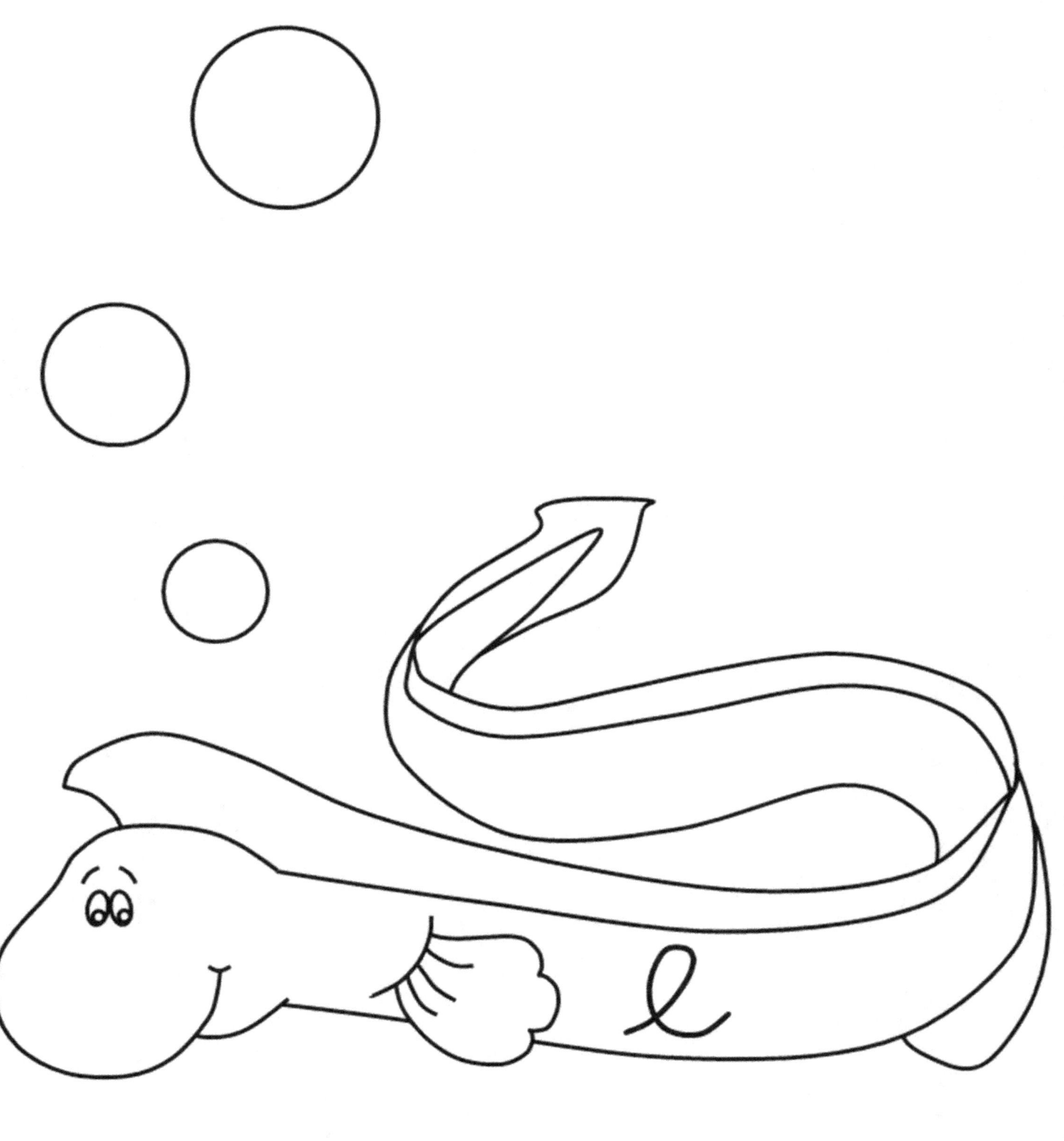

Trace the steps for making the letter e on the following line.

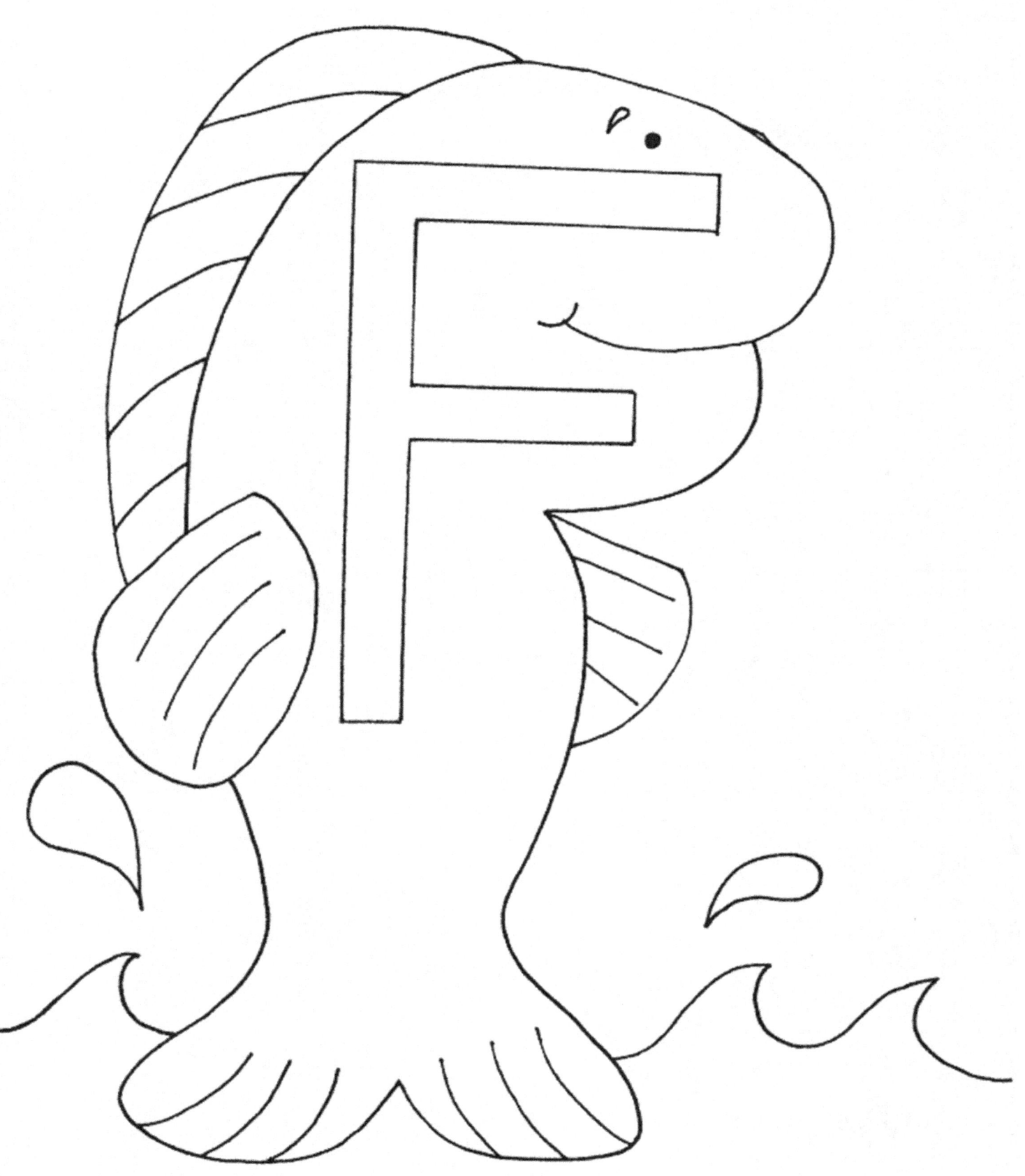

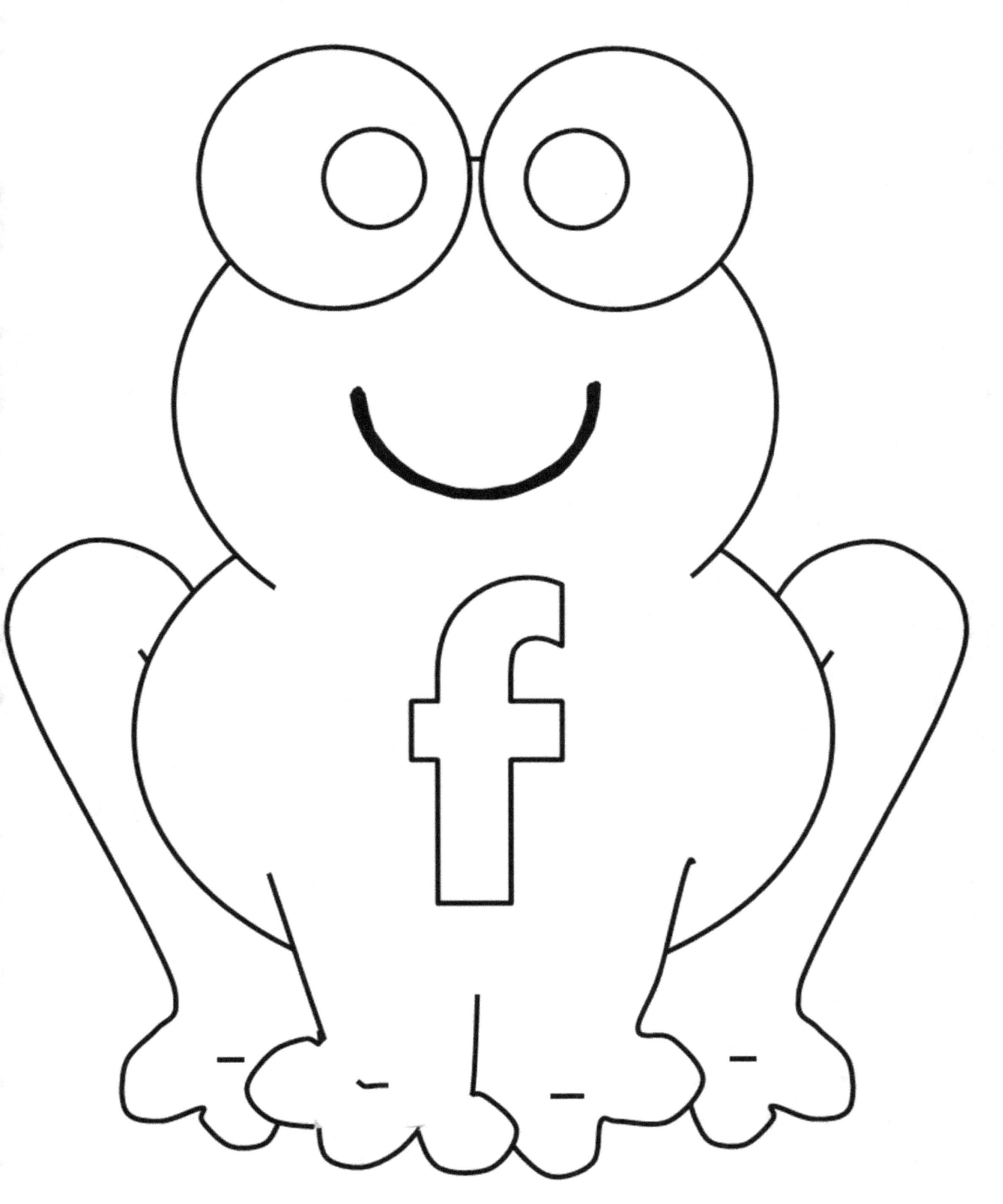

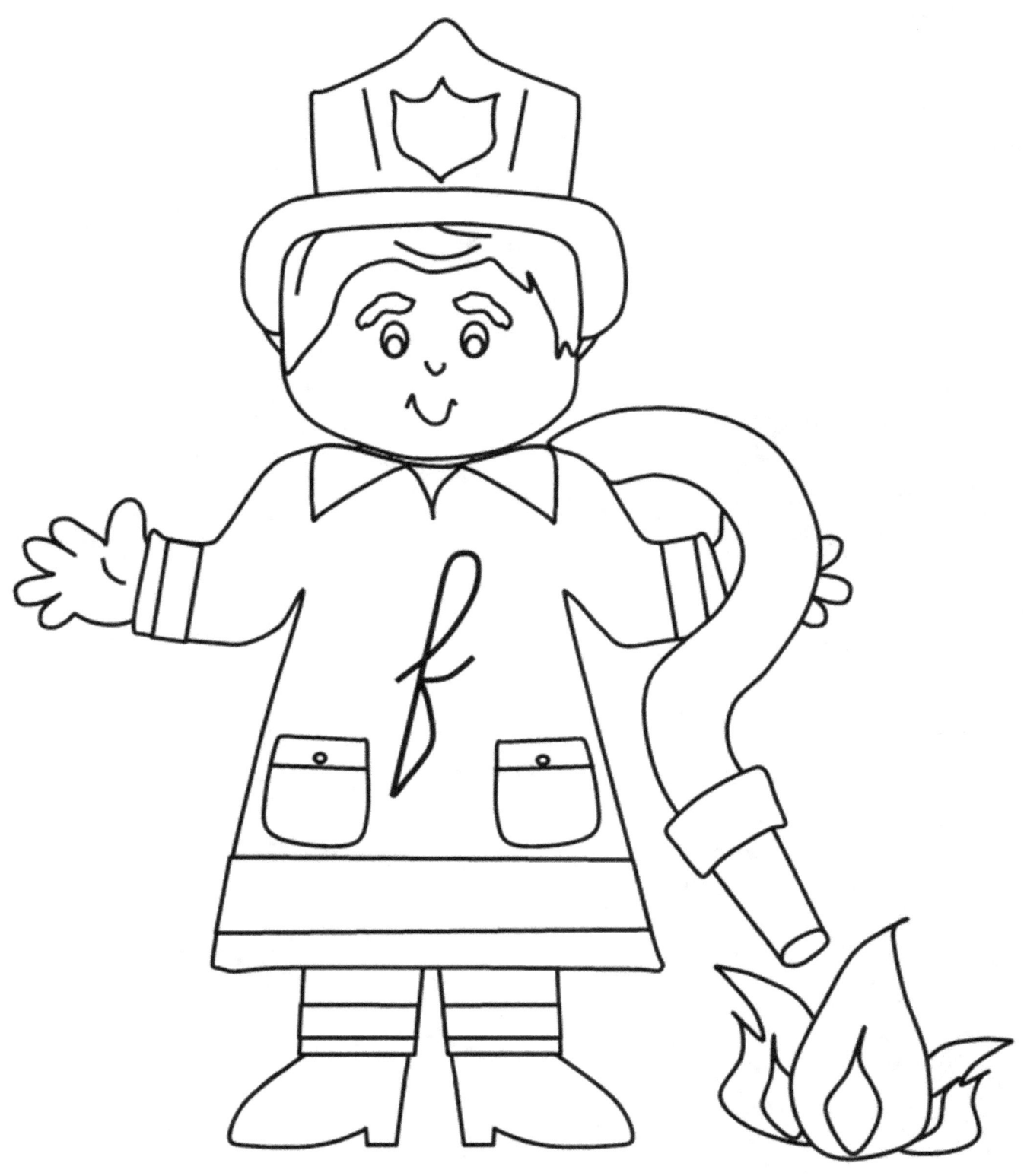

Trace the steps for making the letter f on the following line.

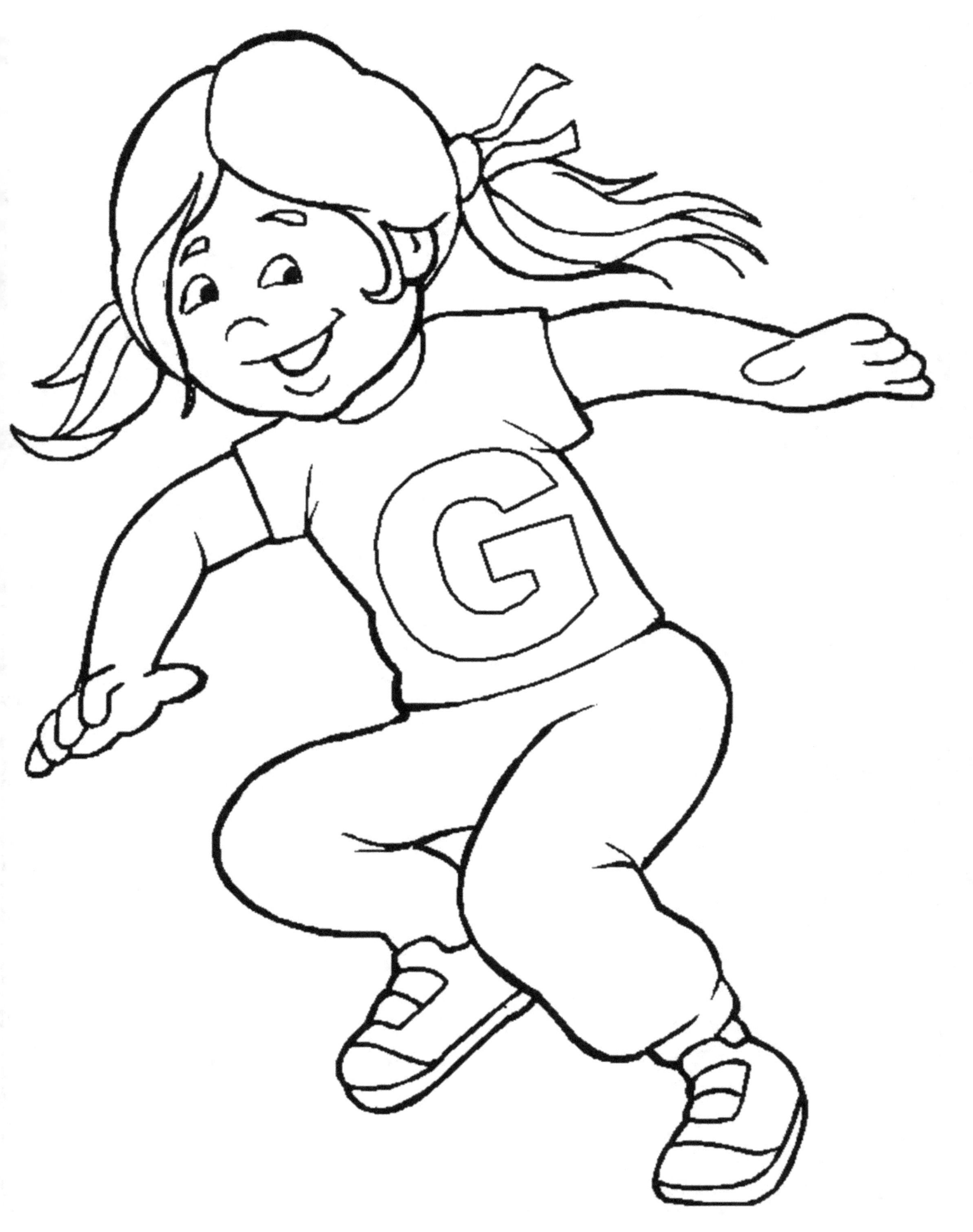

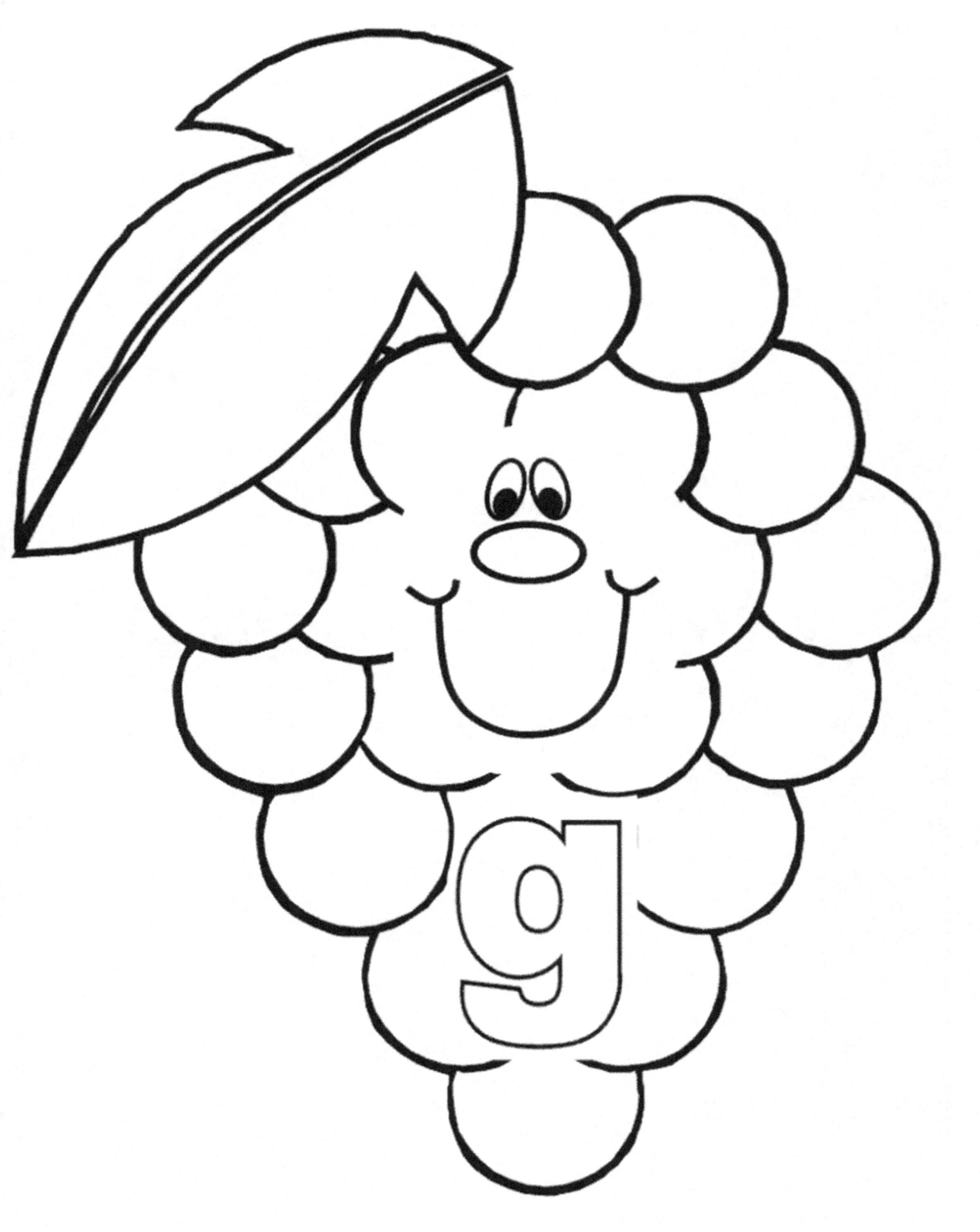

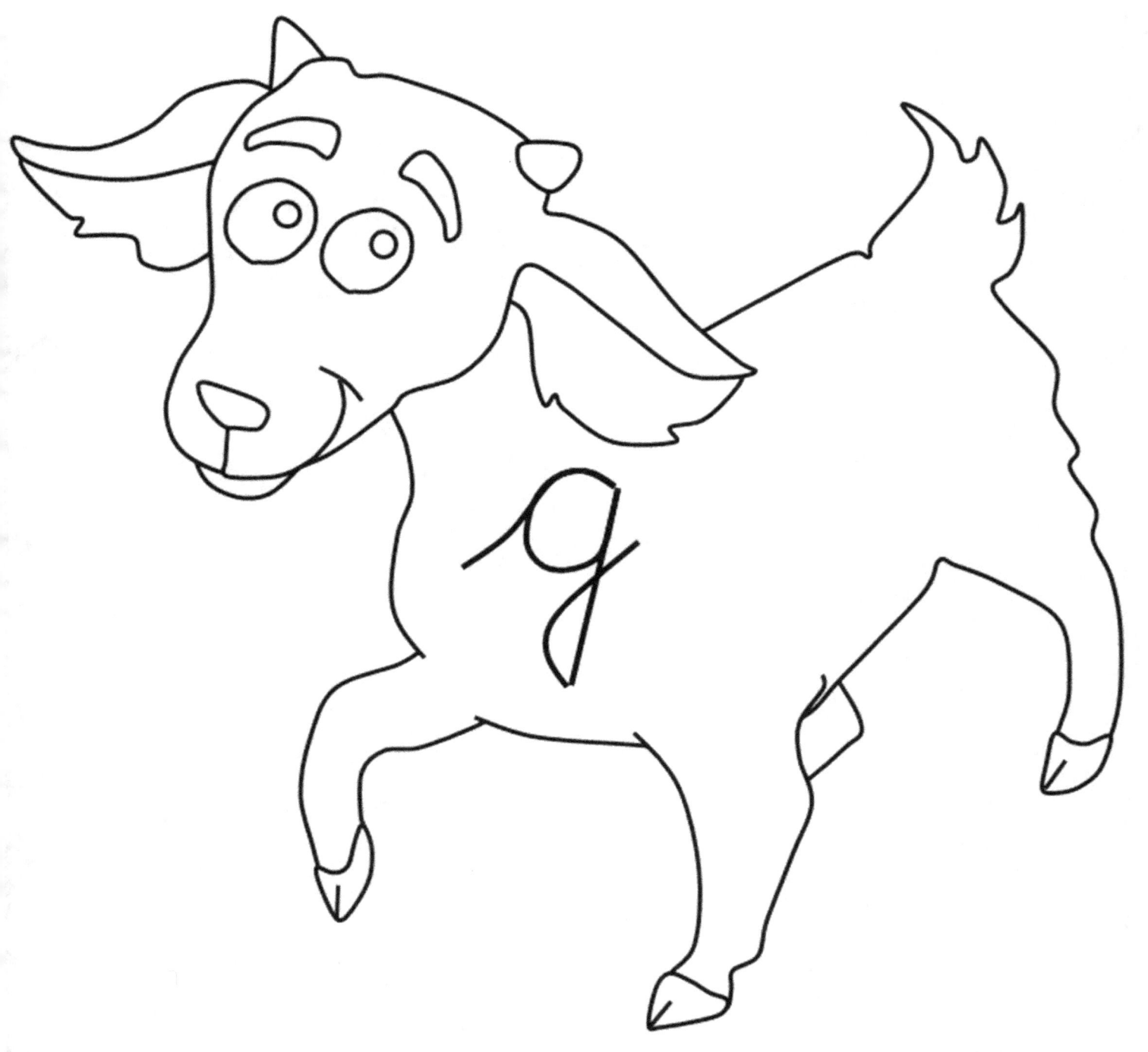

Trace the steps for making the letter g on the following line.

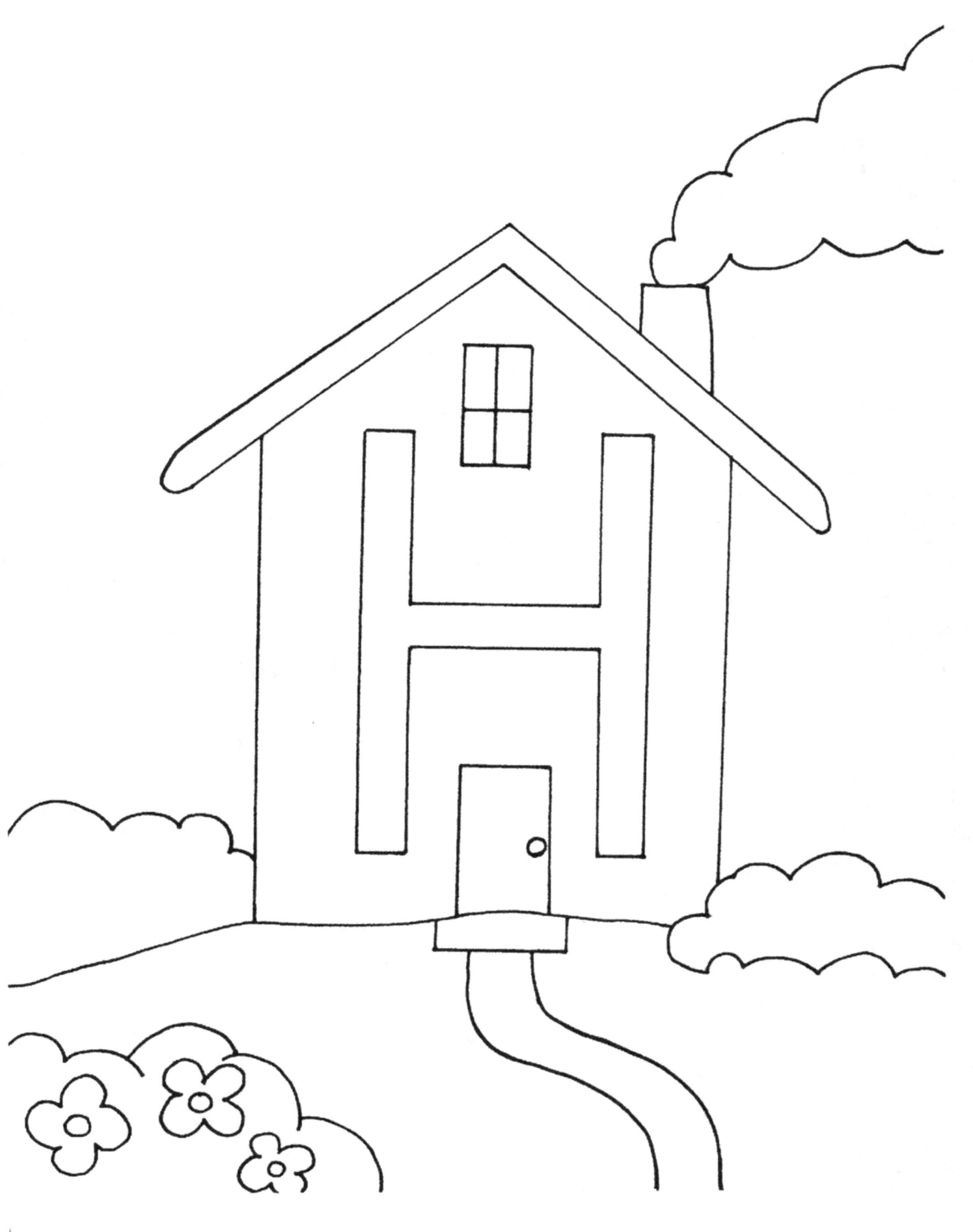

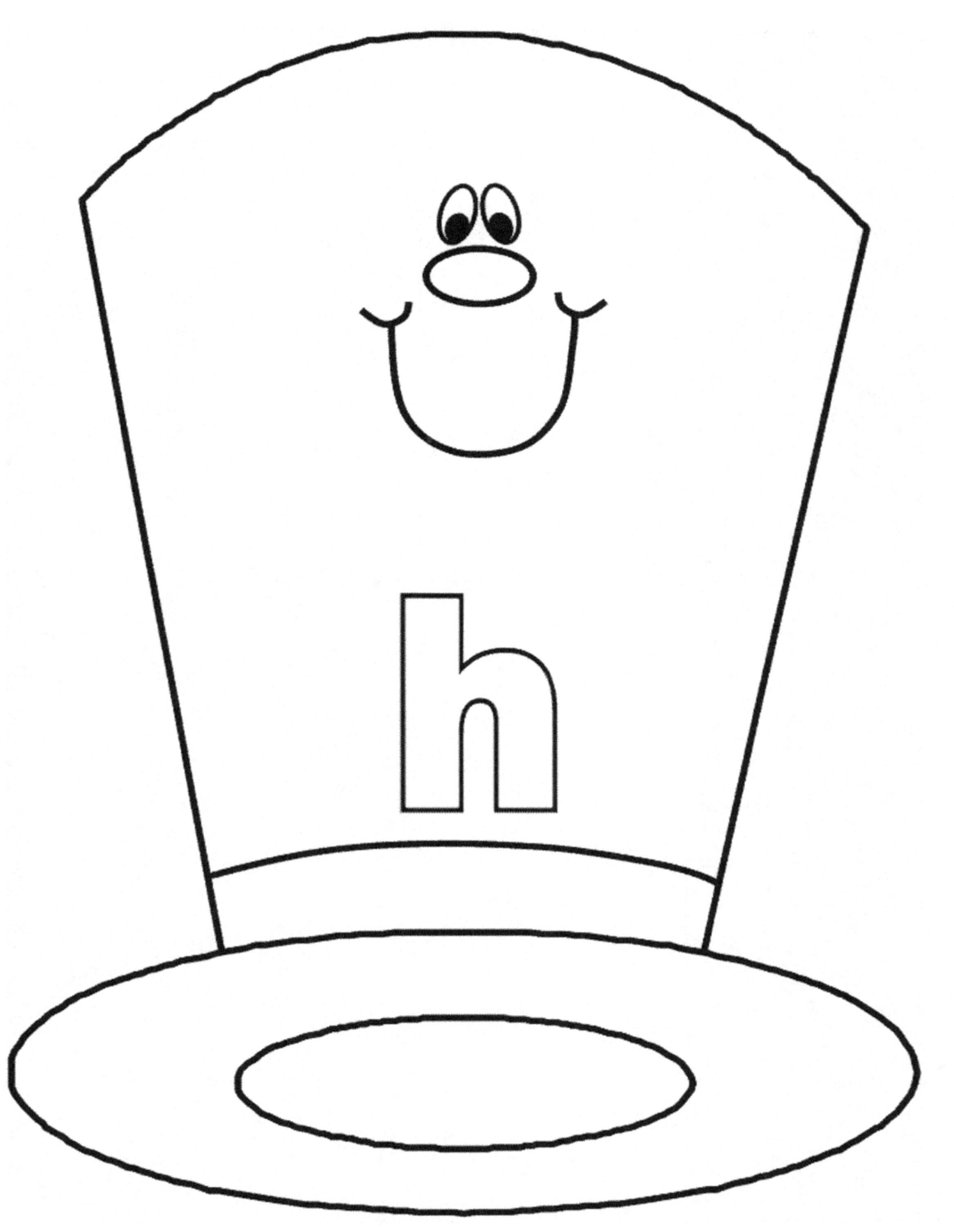

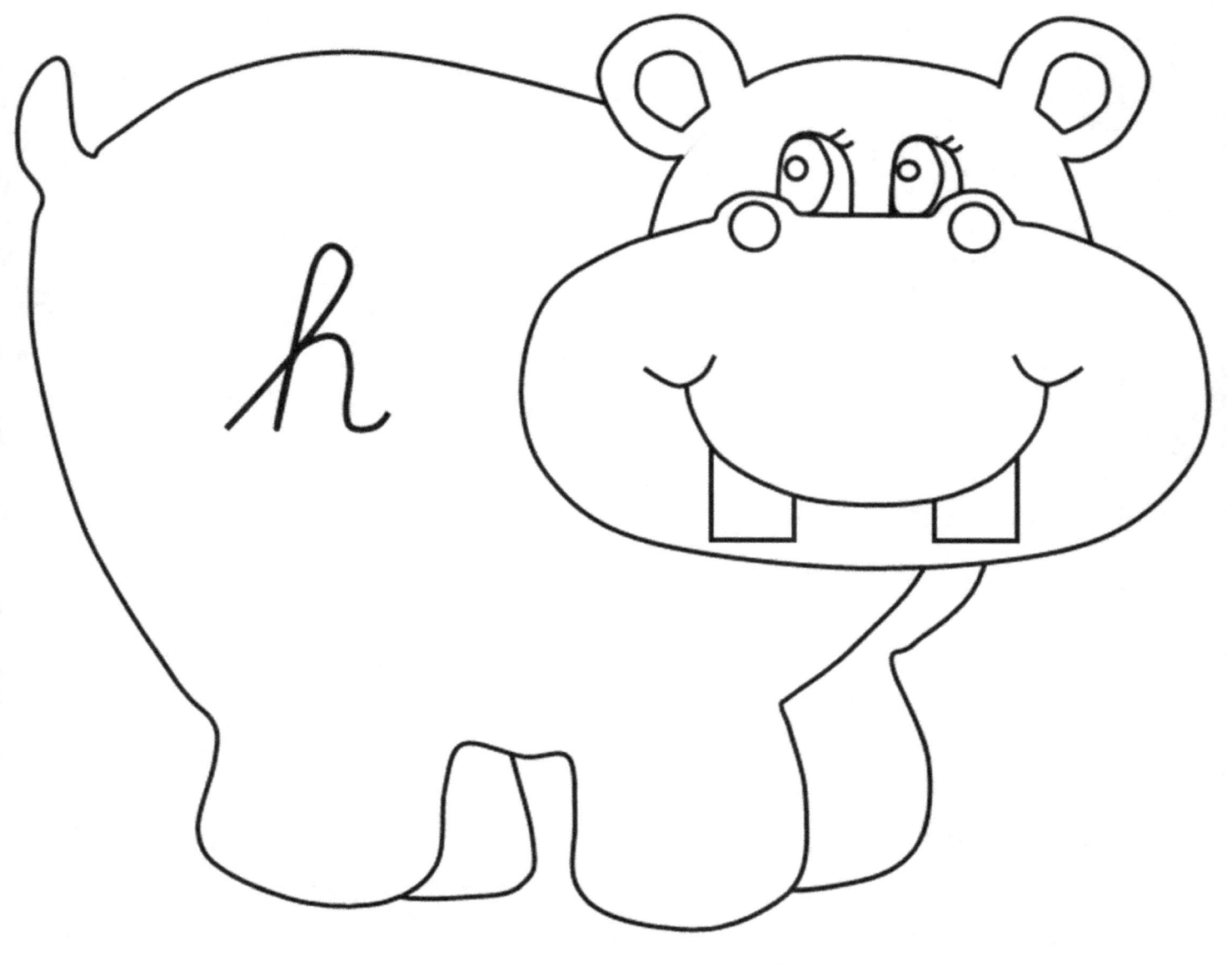

Trace the steps for making the letter h on the following line.

h — h — h — h — h — hh

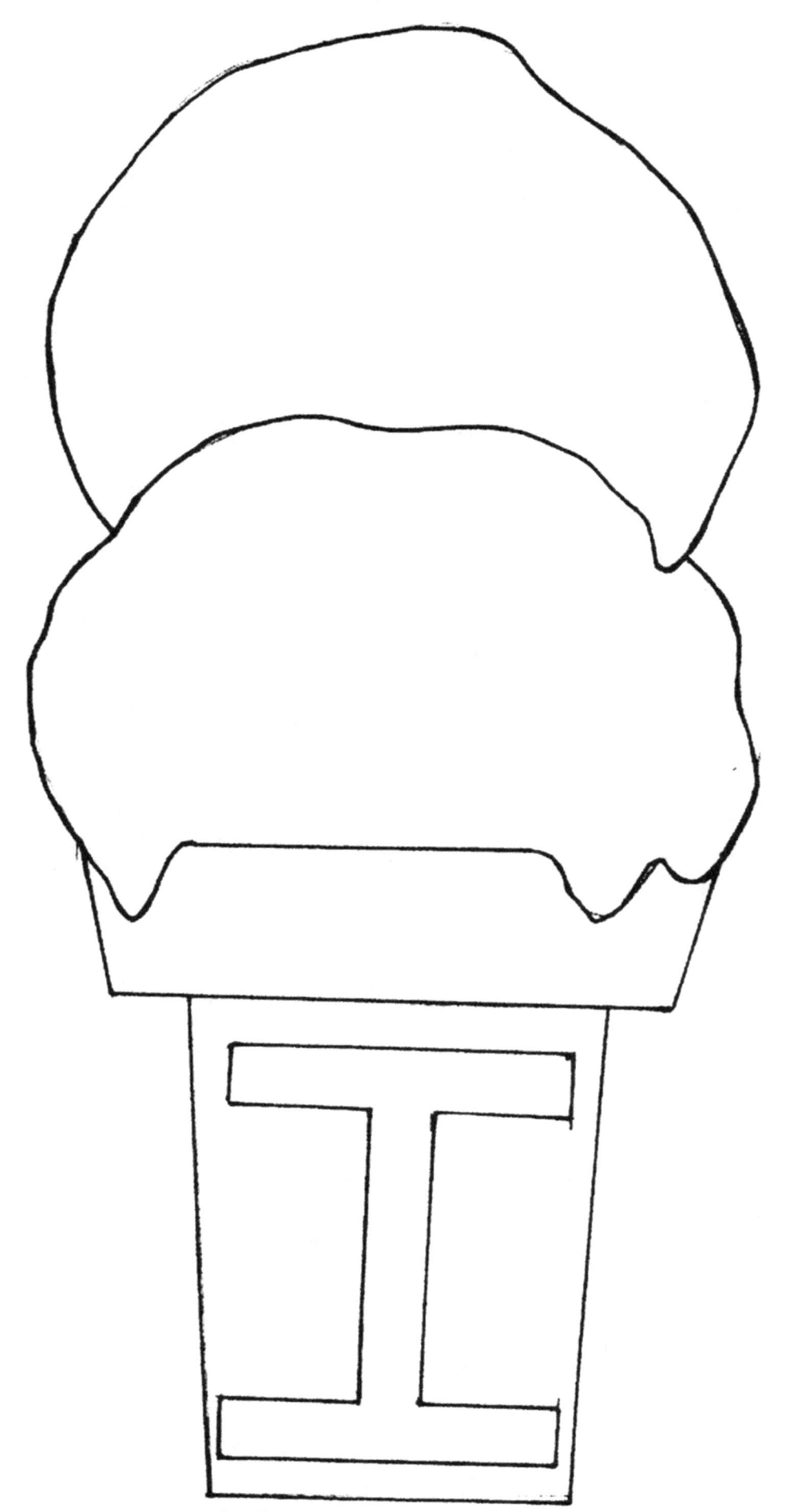

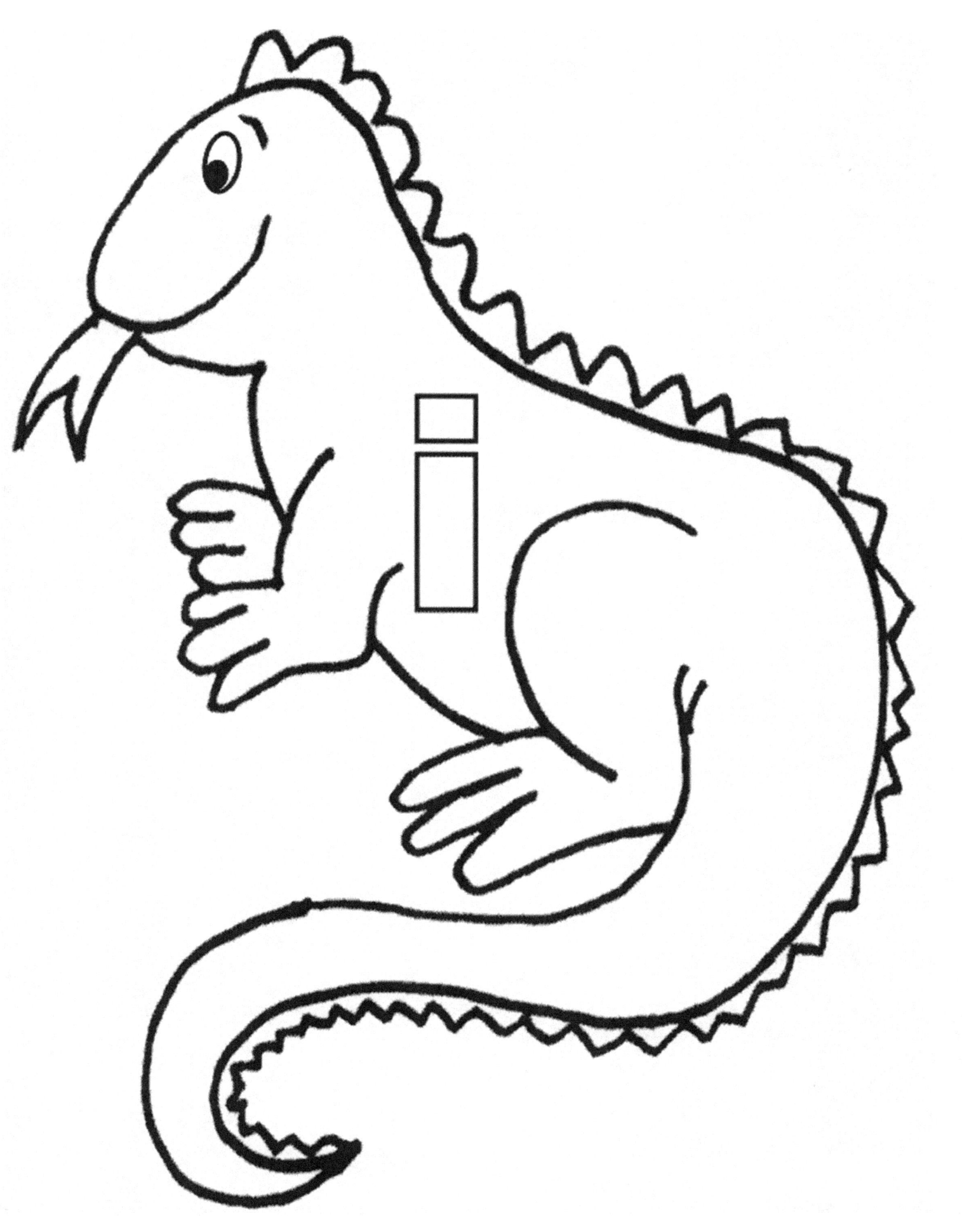

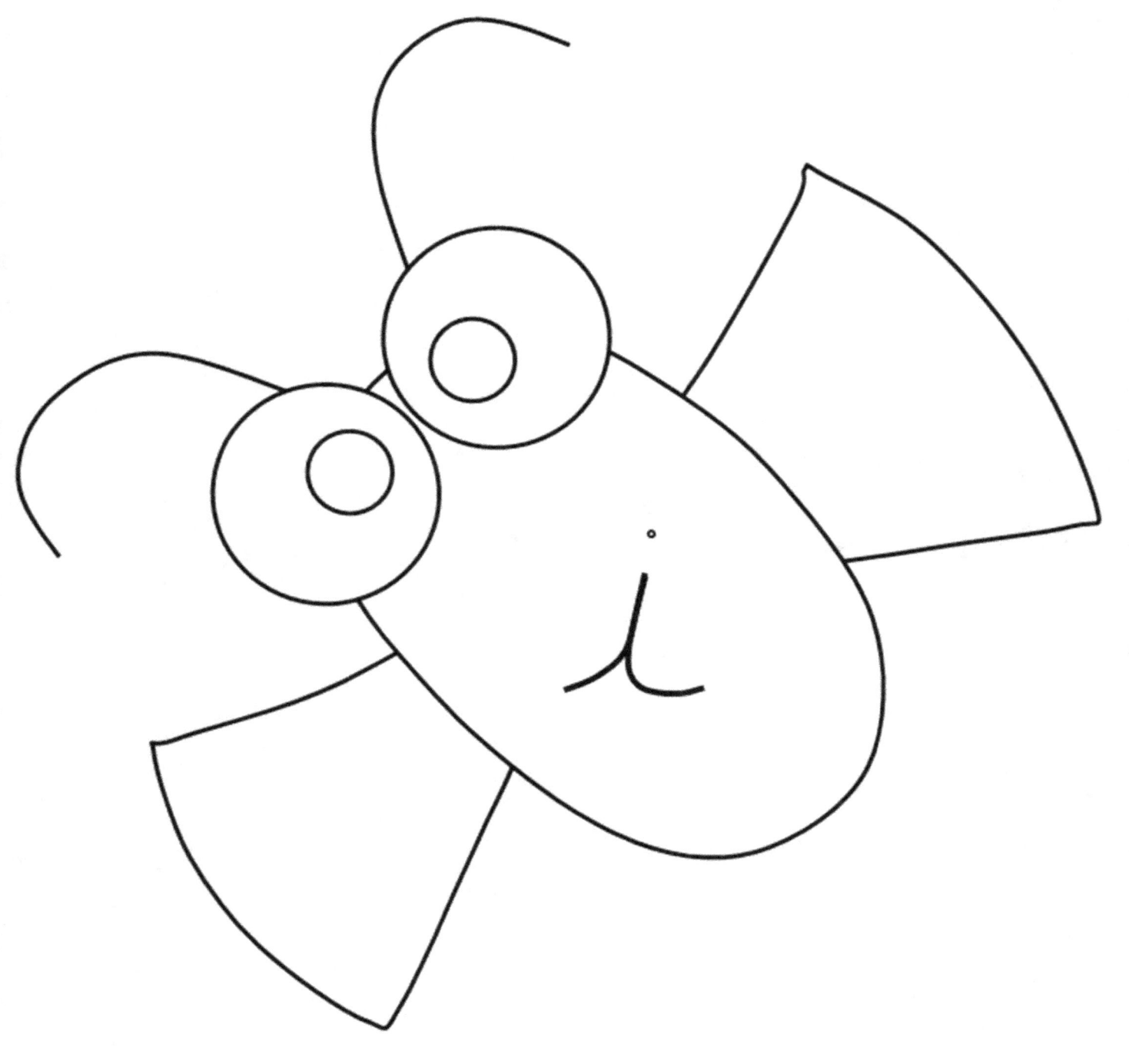

Trace the steps for making the letter i on the following line.

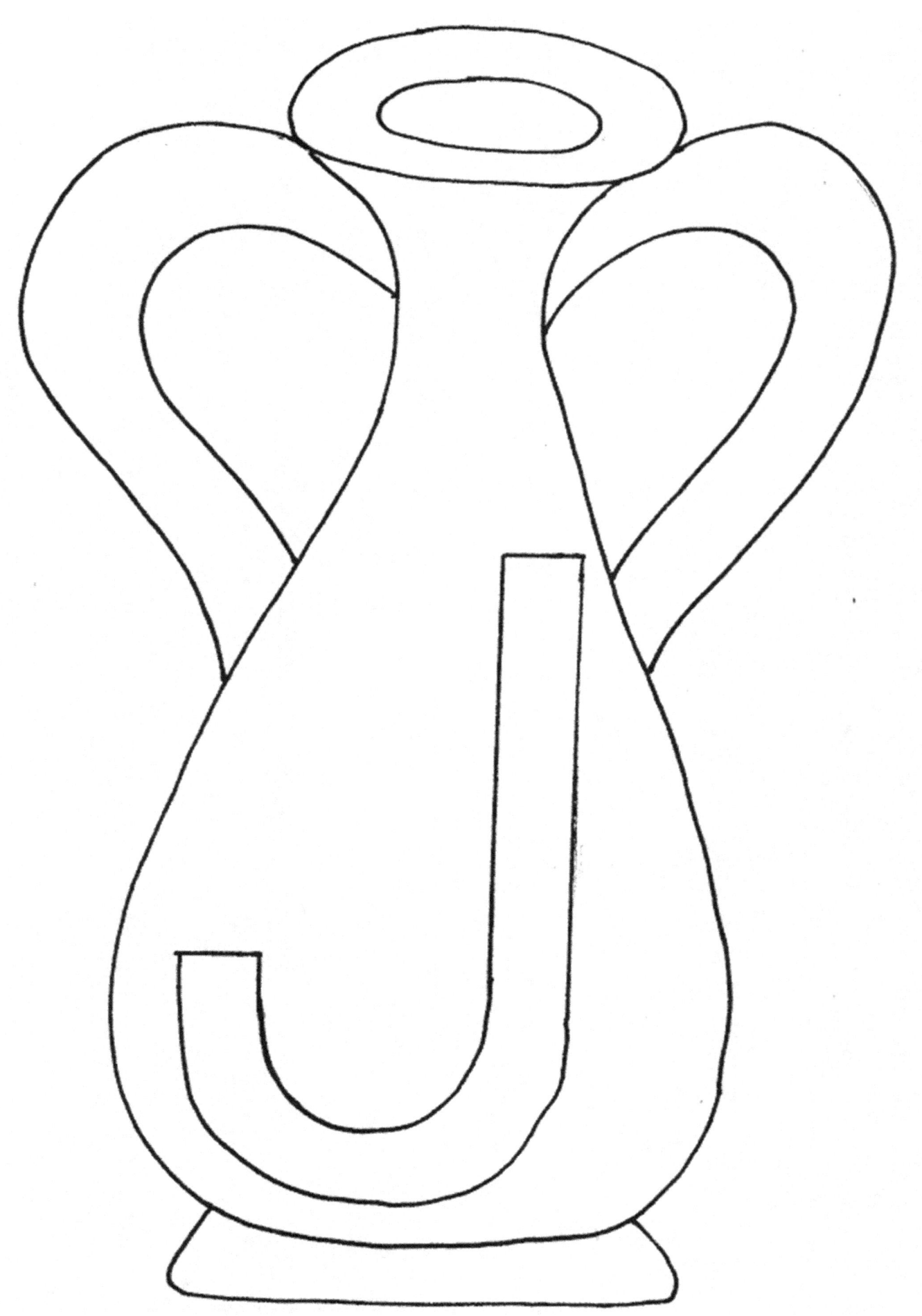

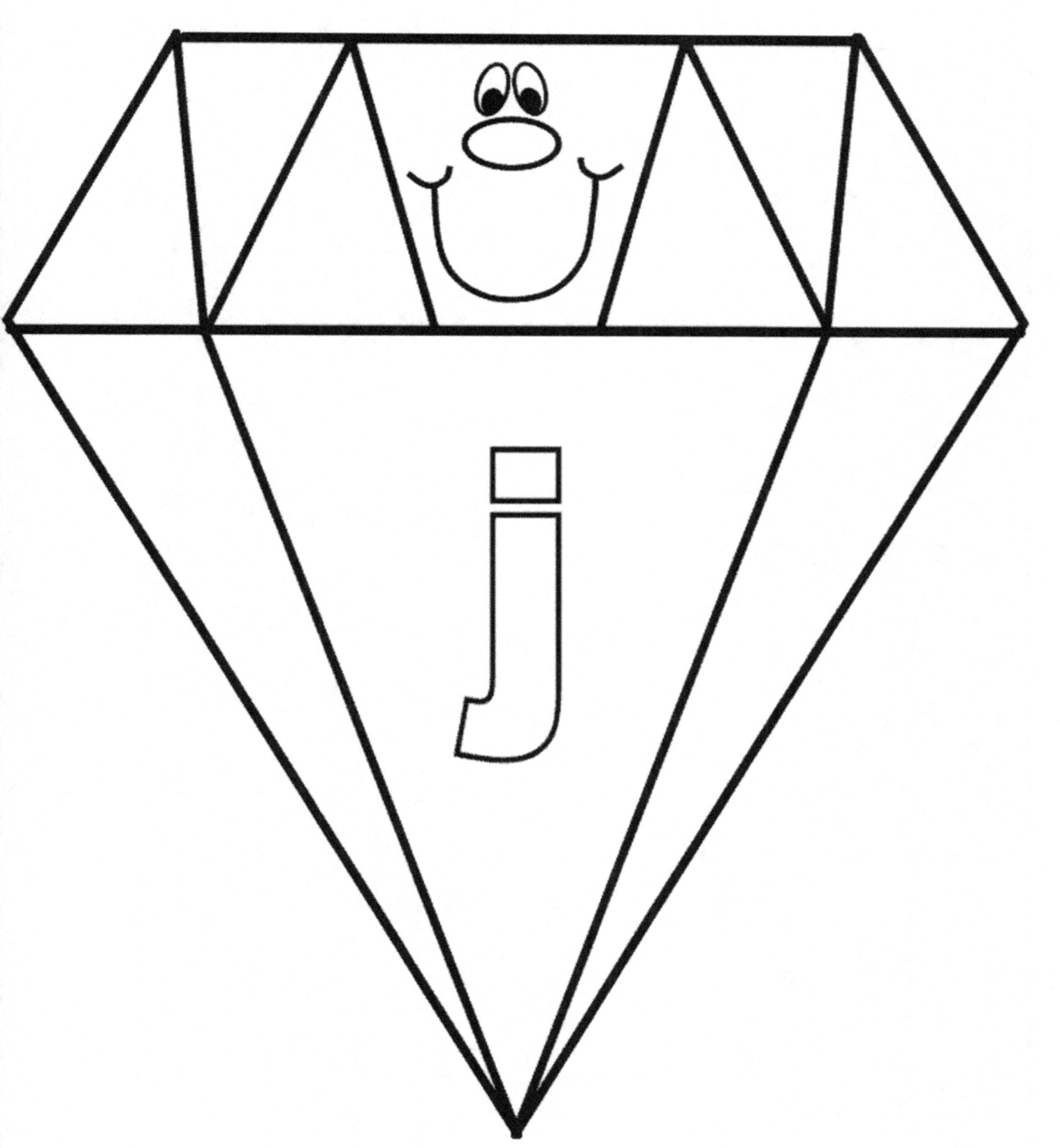

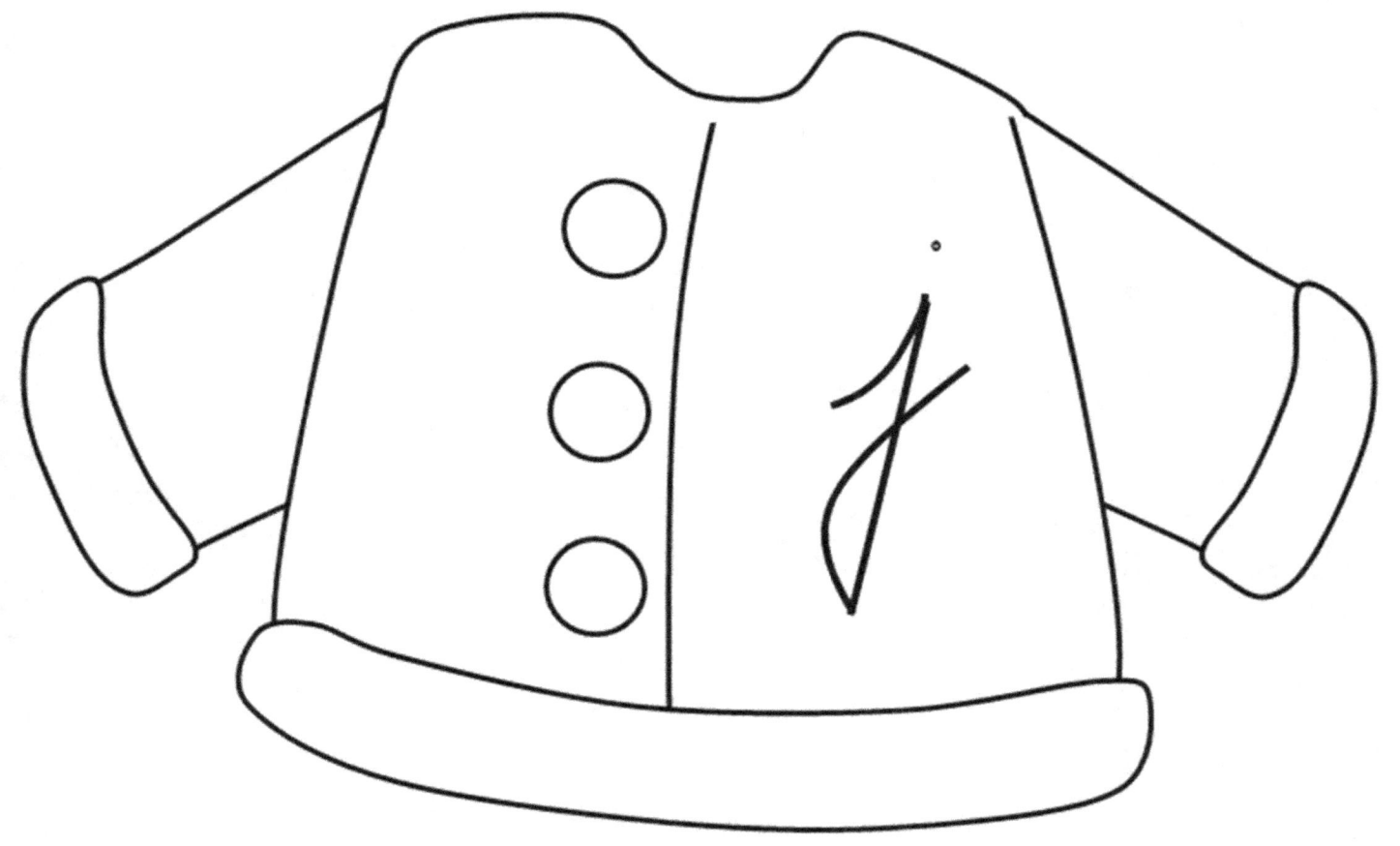

Trace the steps for making the letter j on the following line.

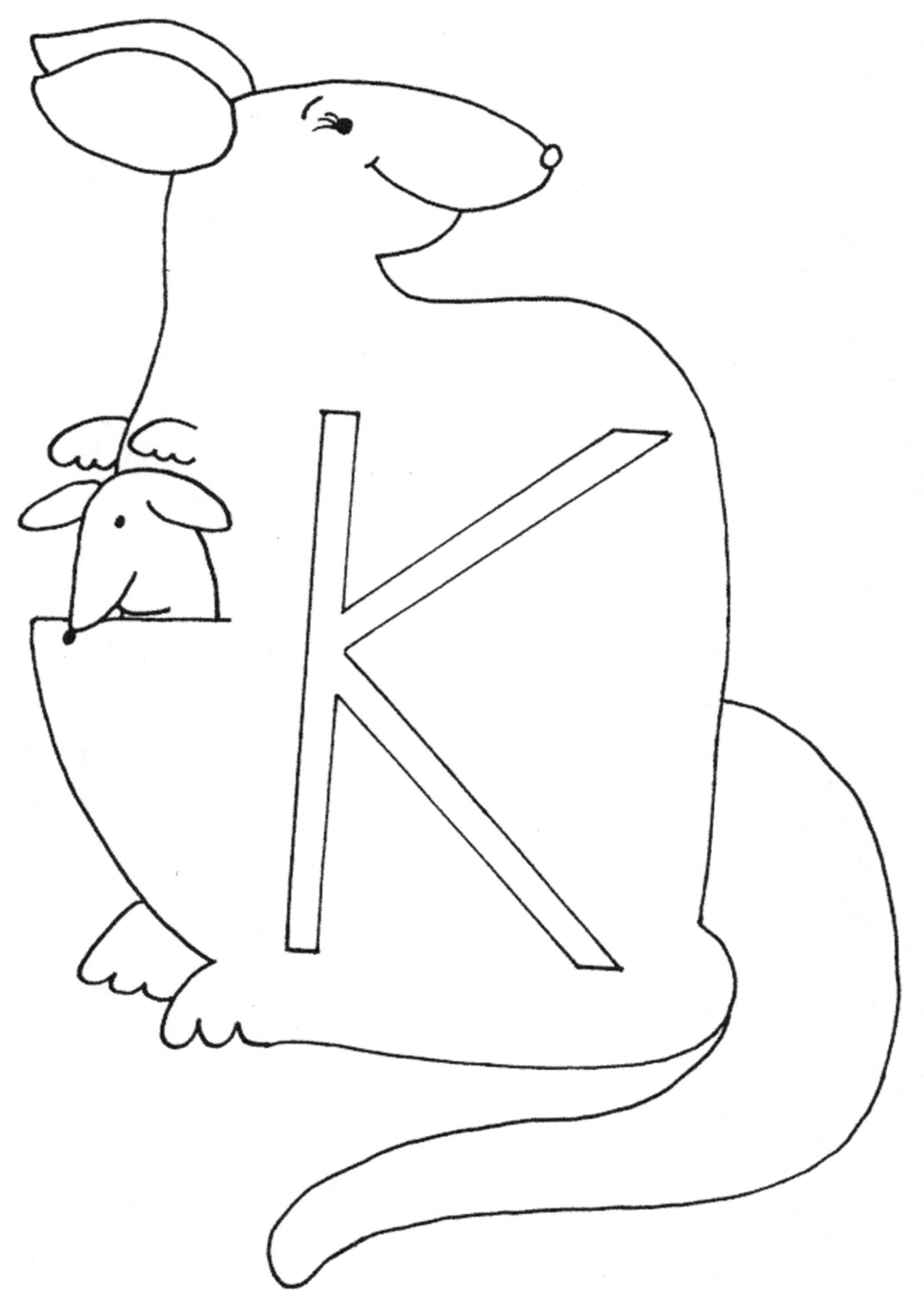

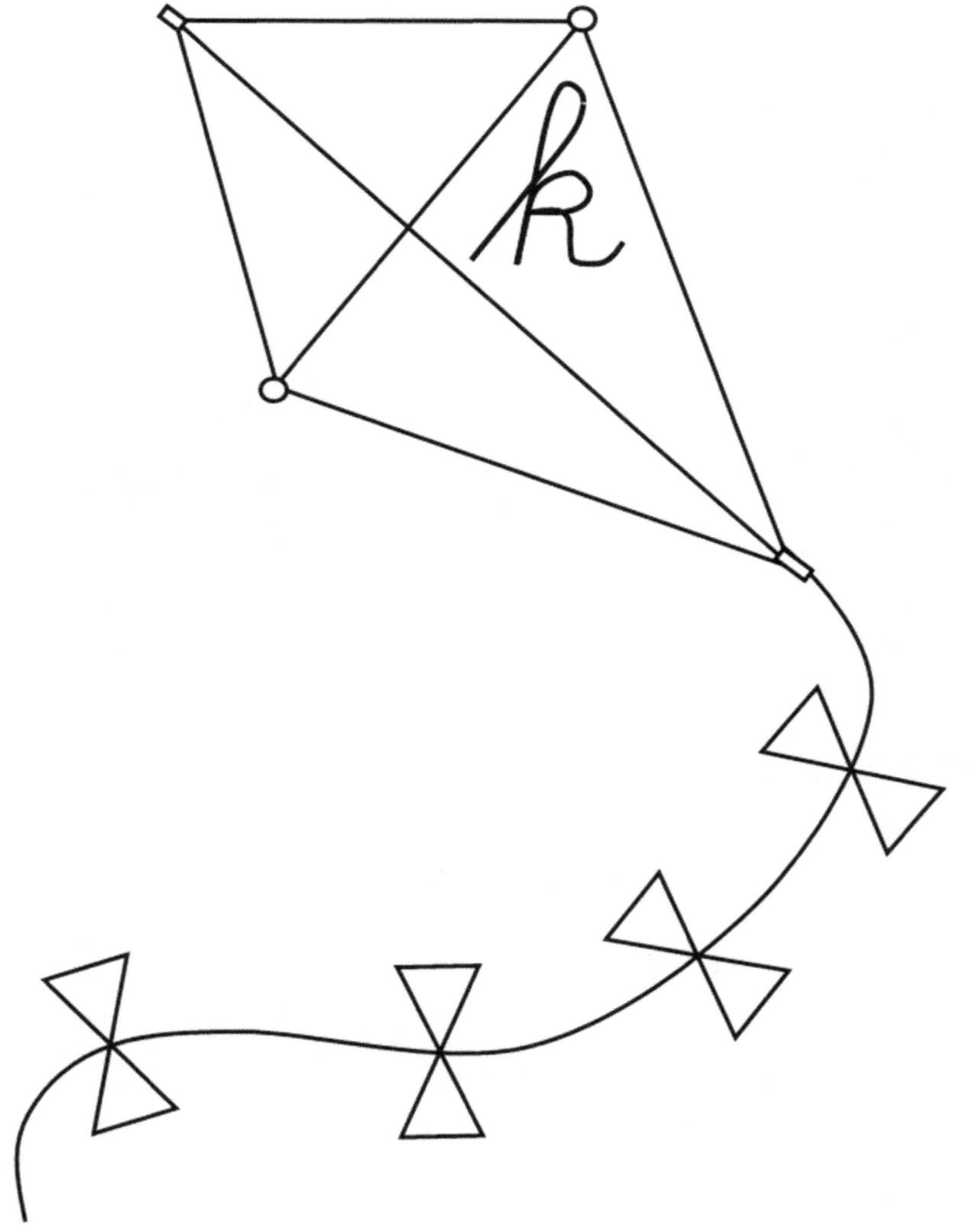

Trace the steps for making the letter k on the following line.

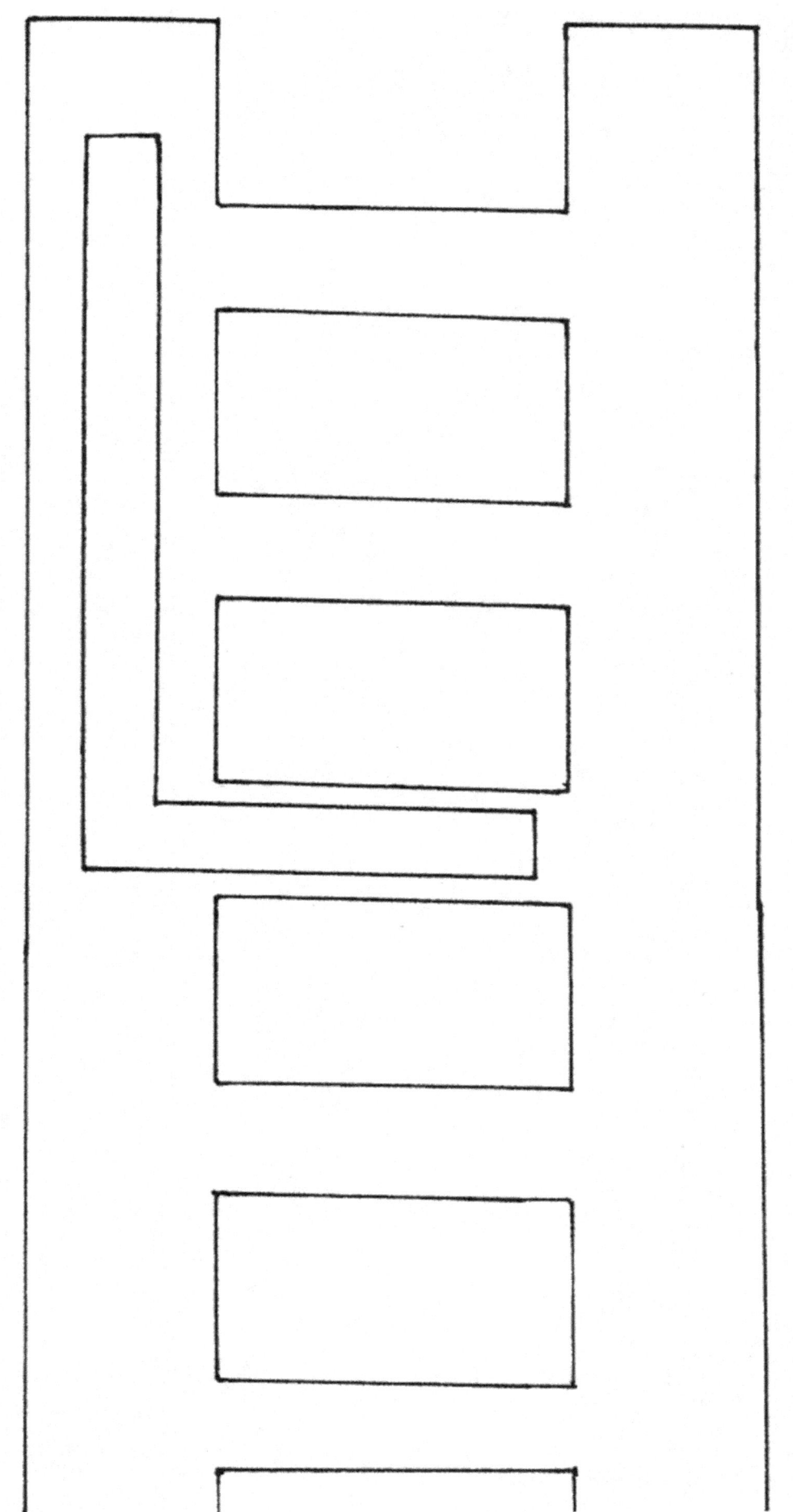

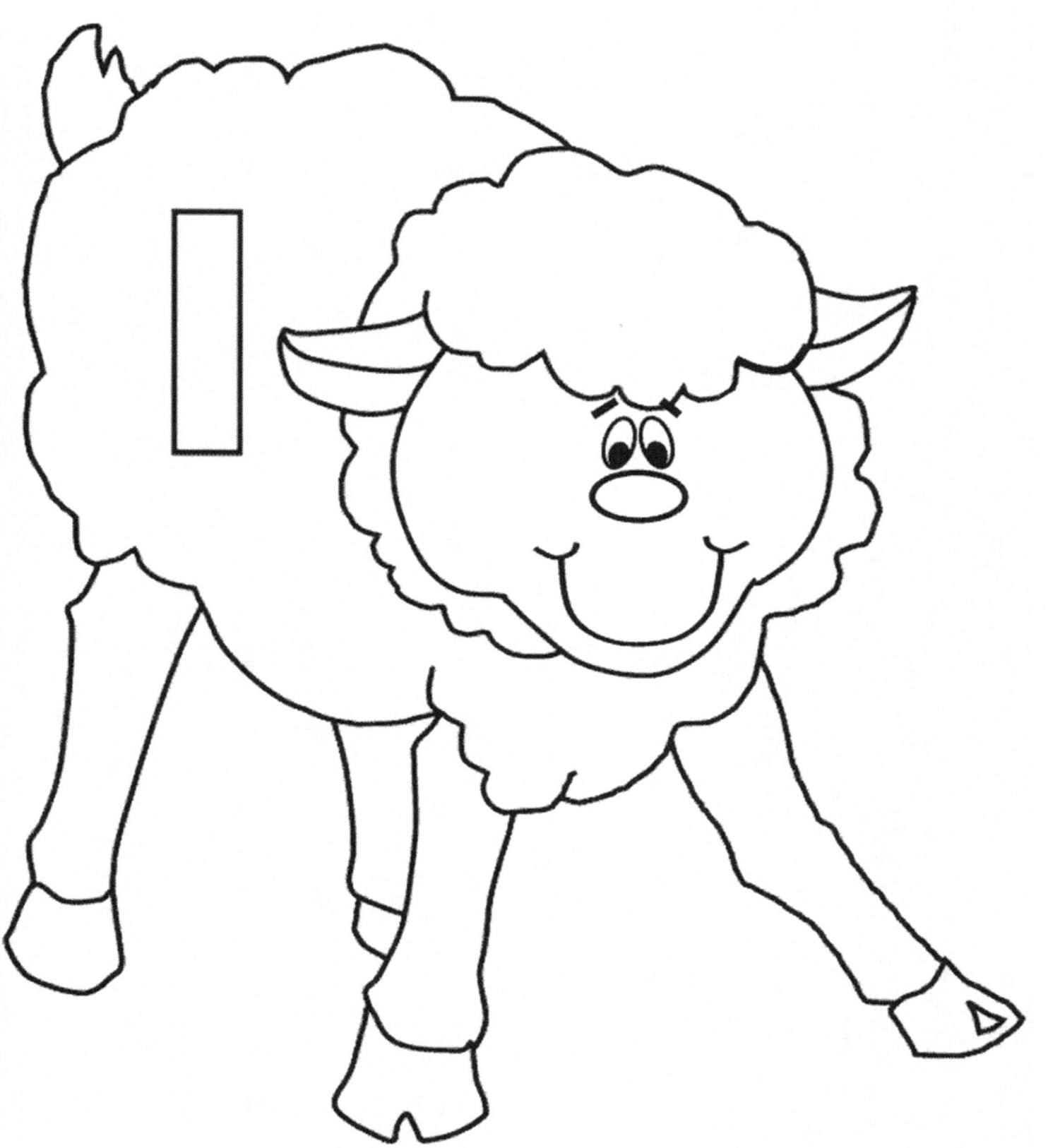

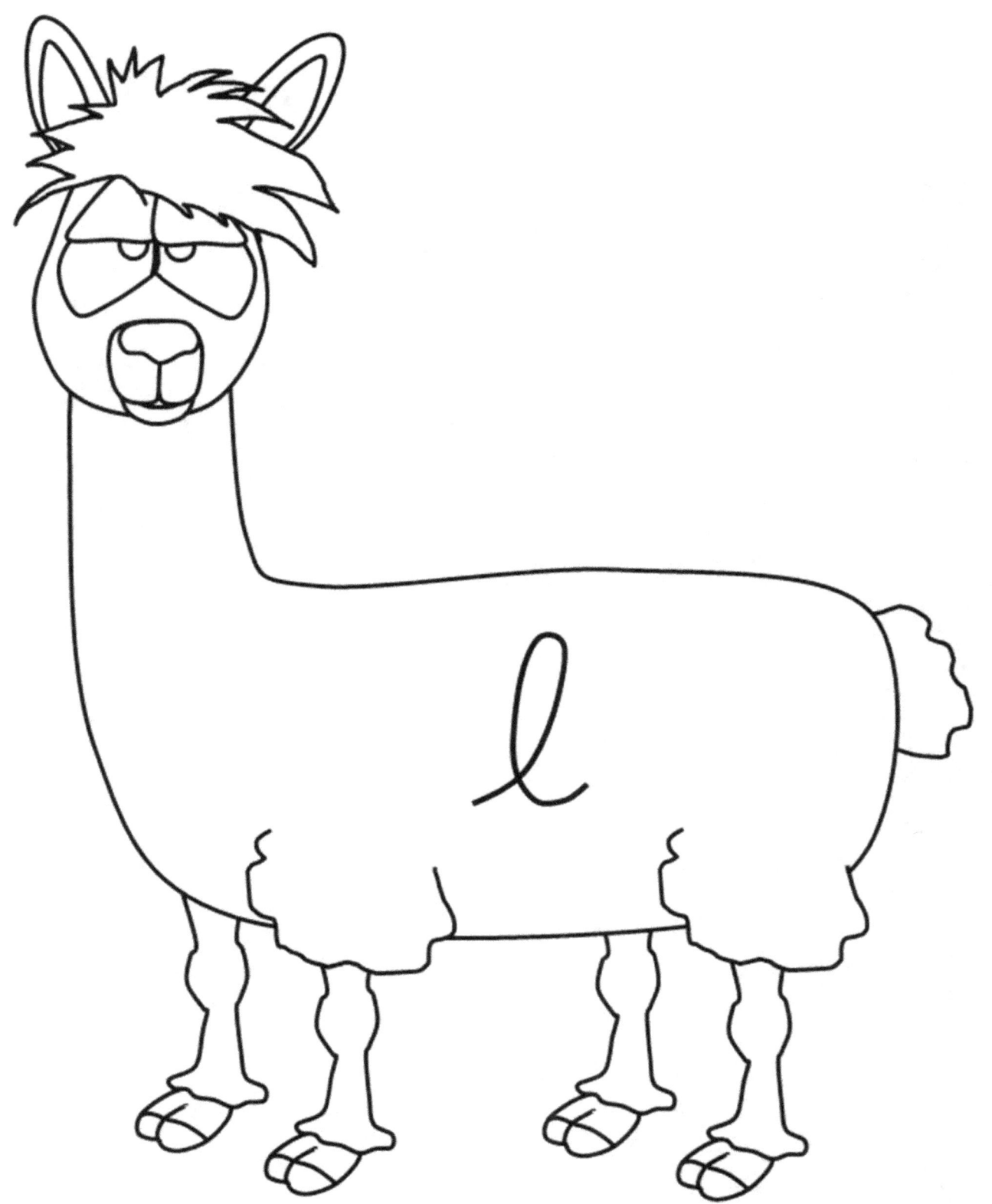

Trace the steps for making the letter l on the following line.

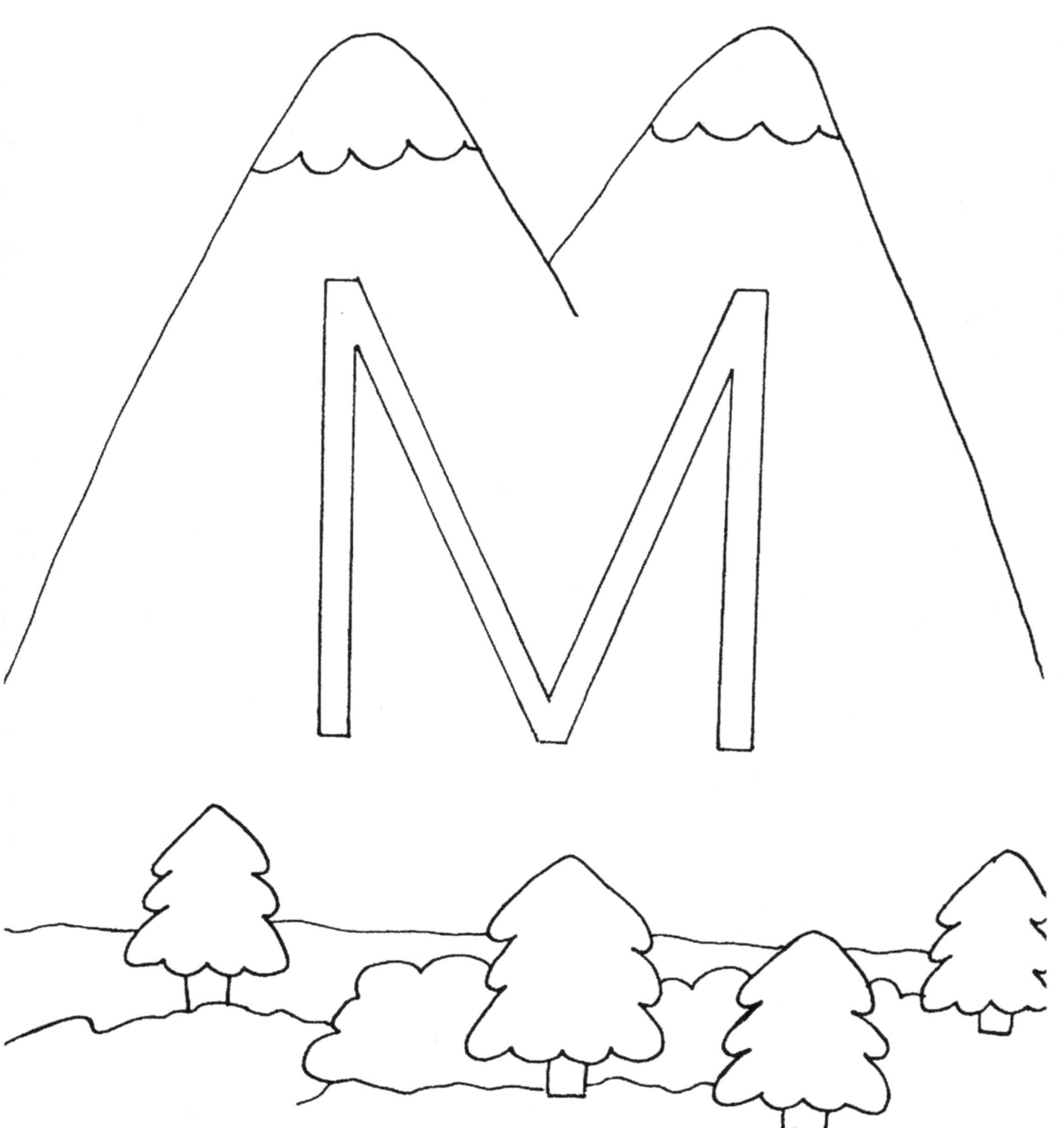

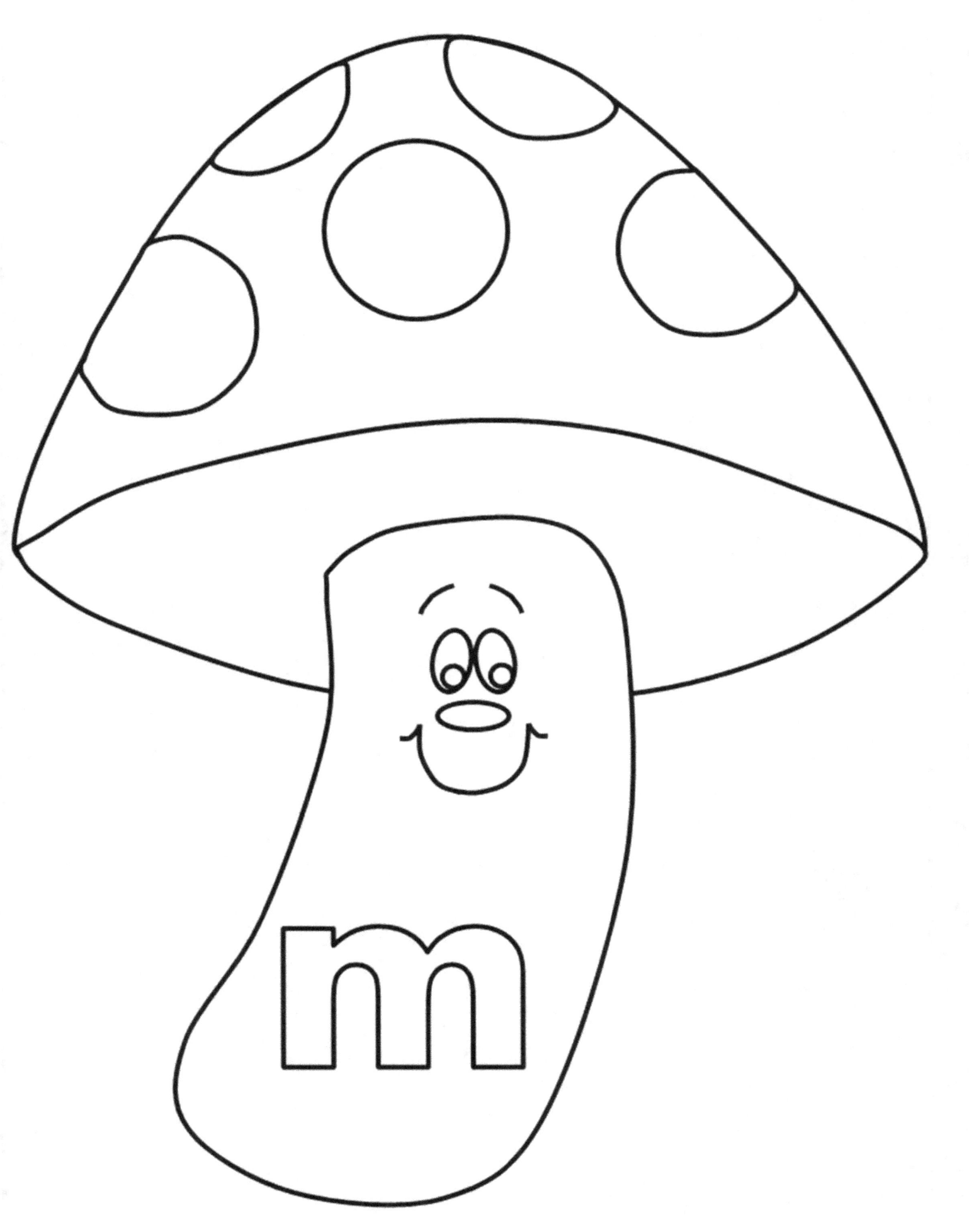

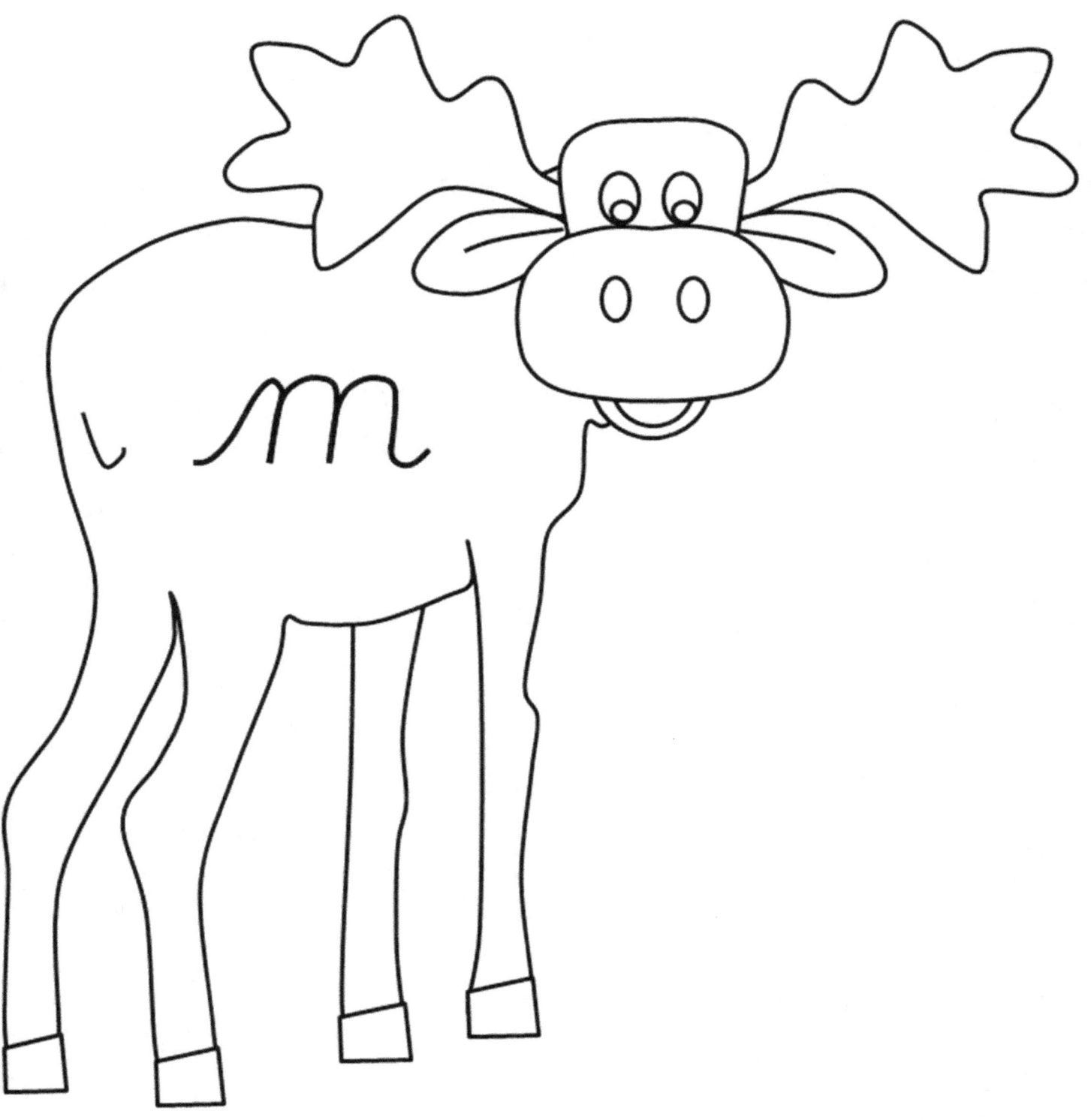

Trace the steps for making the letter m on the following line.

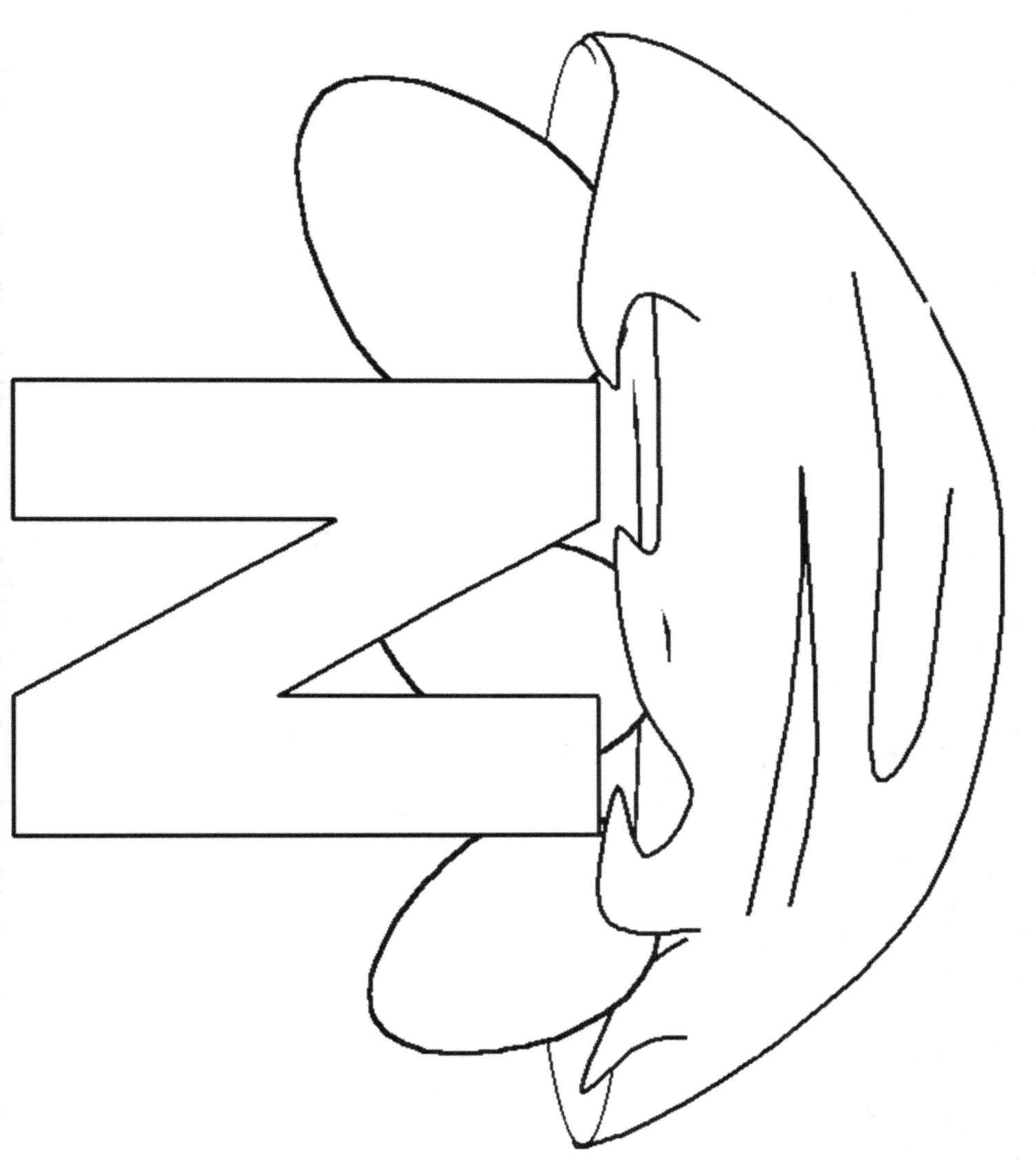

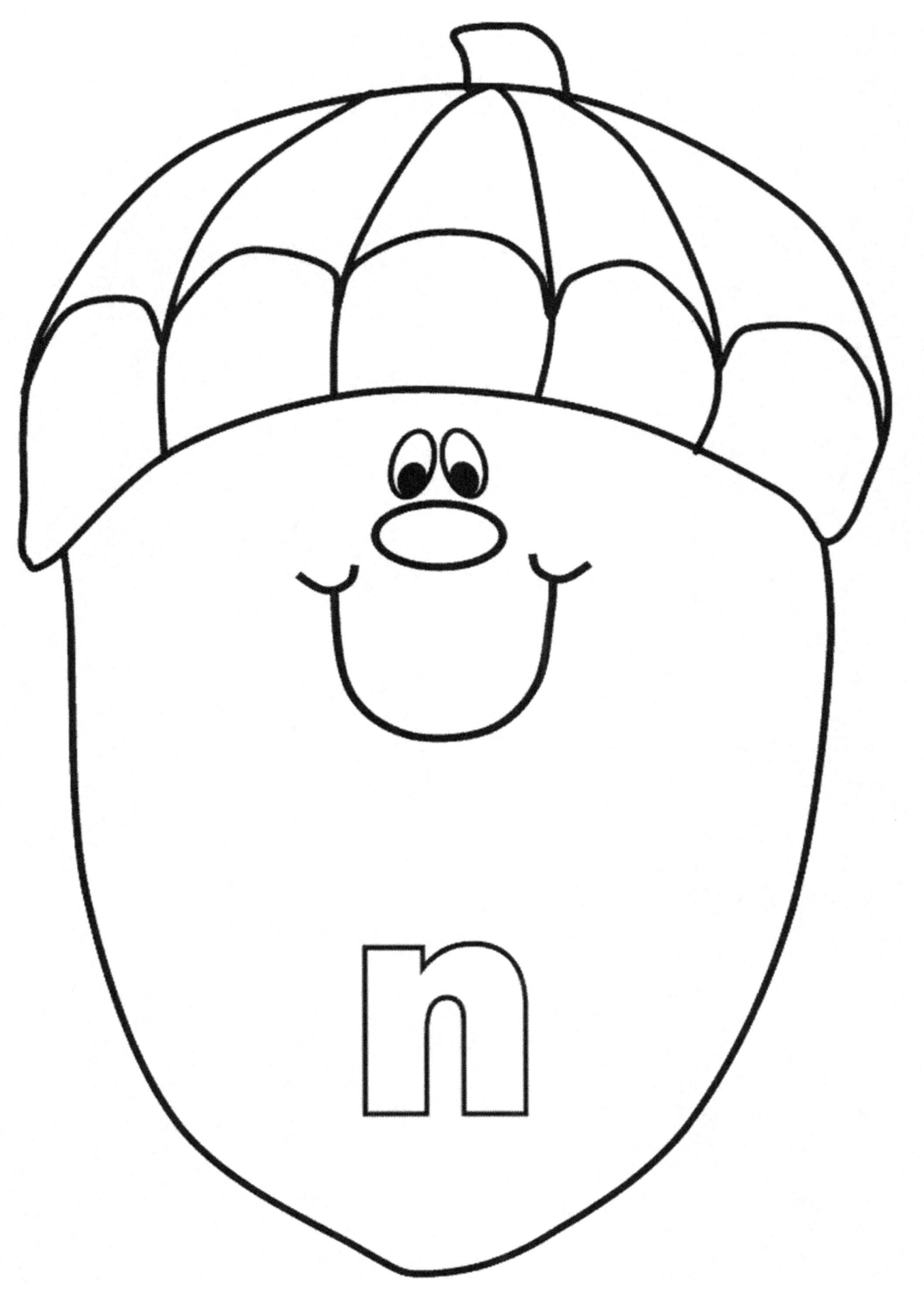

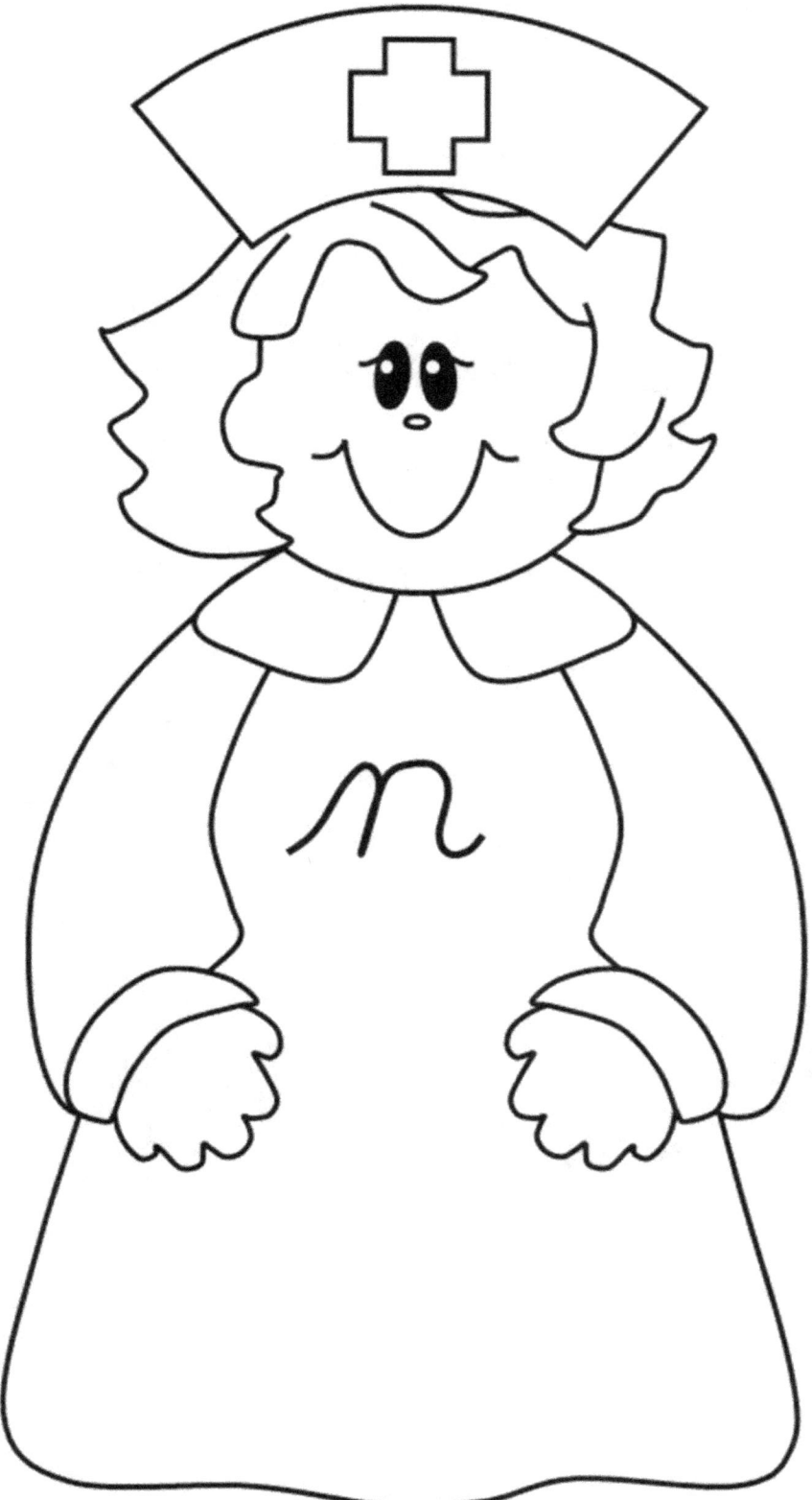

Trace the steps for making the letter n on the following line.

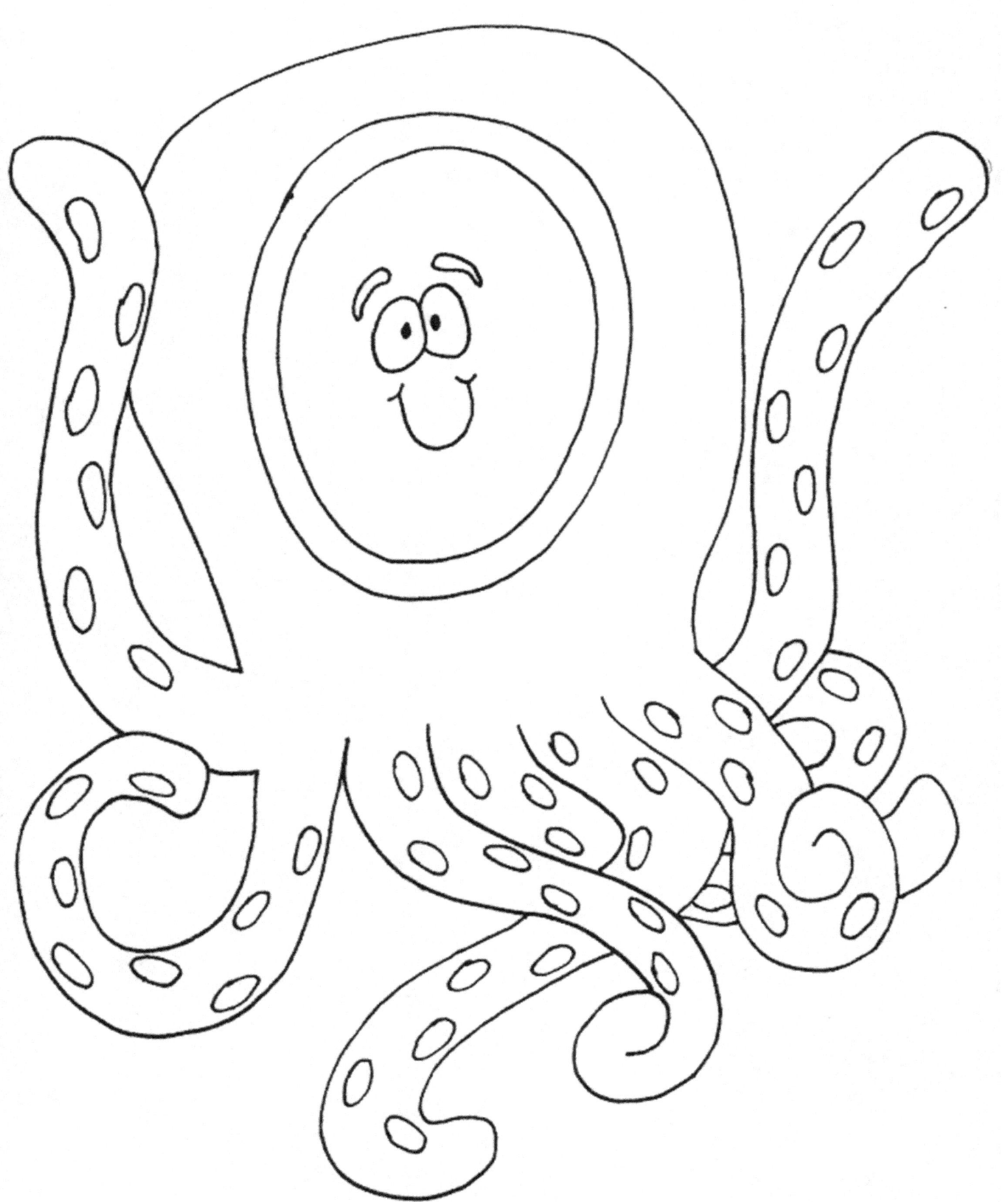

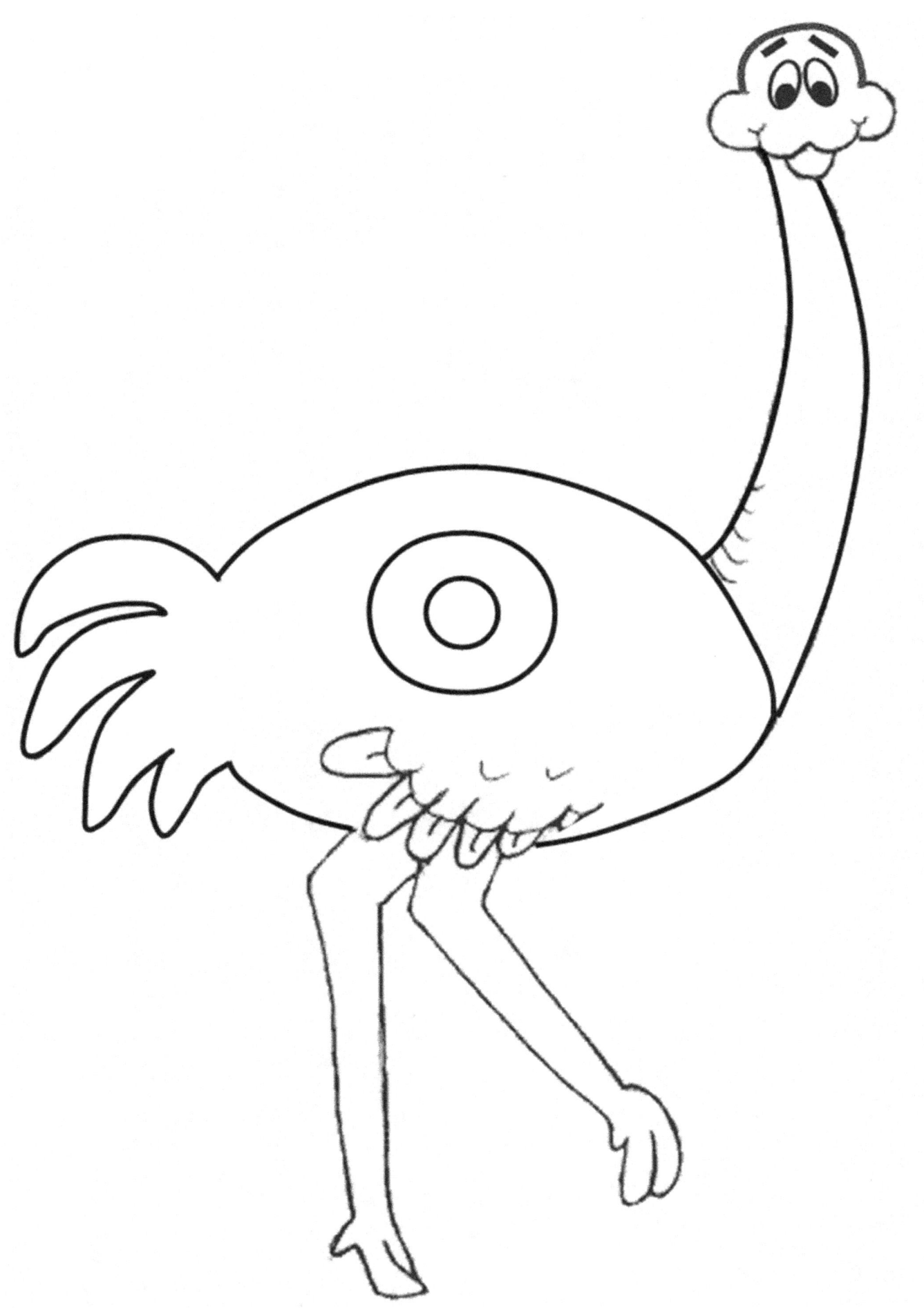

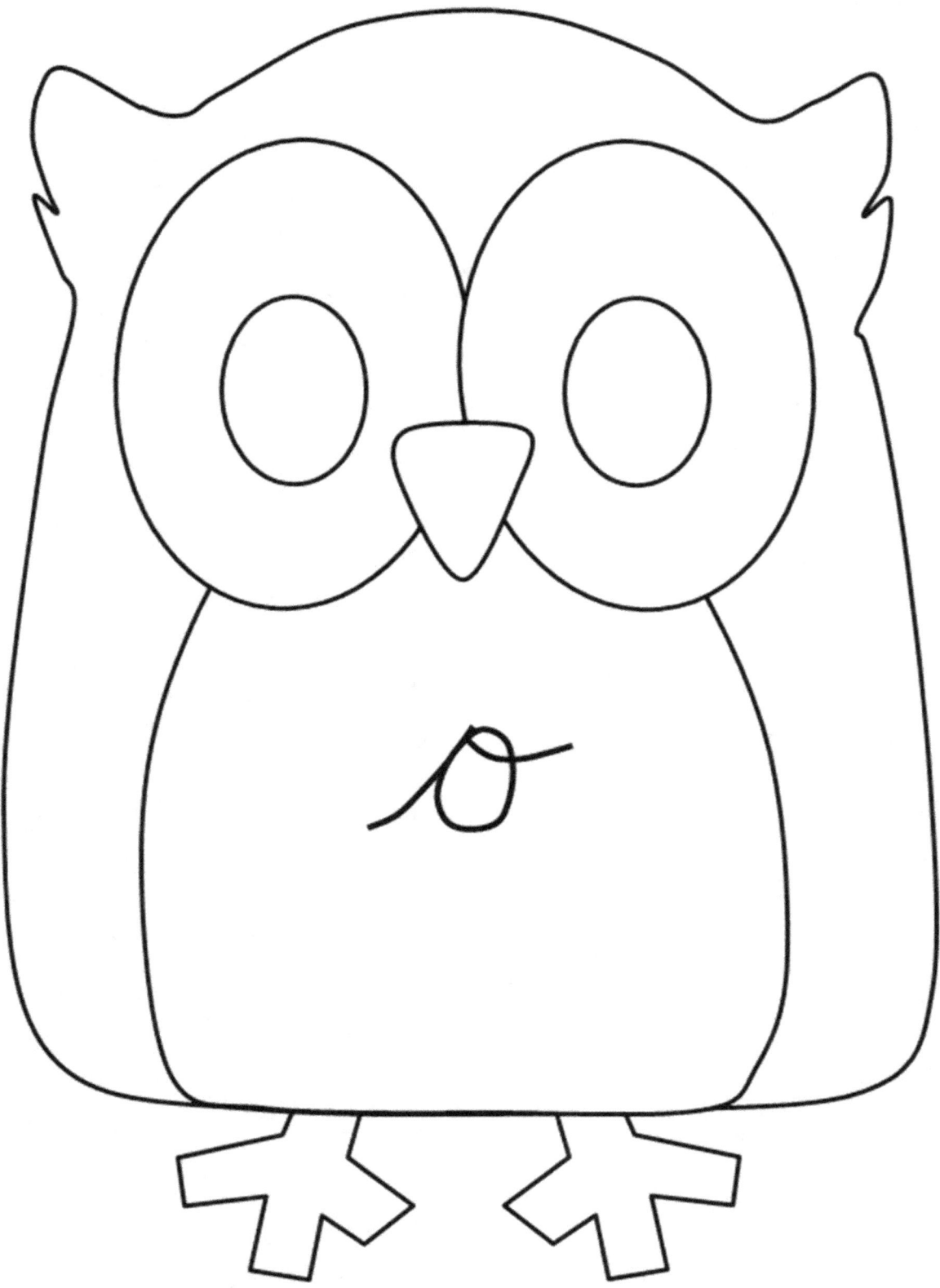

Trace the steps for making the letter o on the following line.

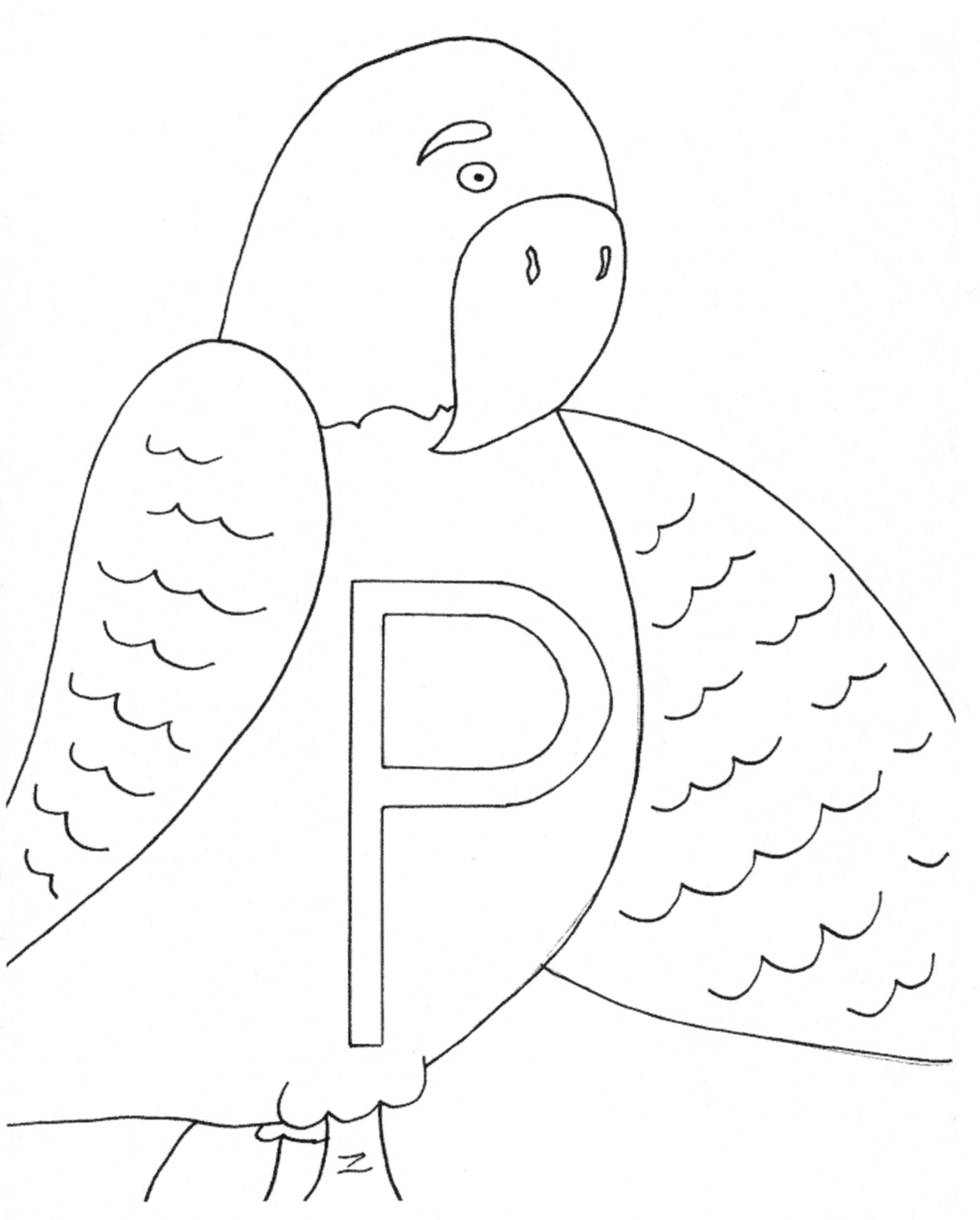

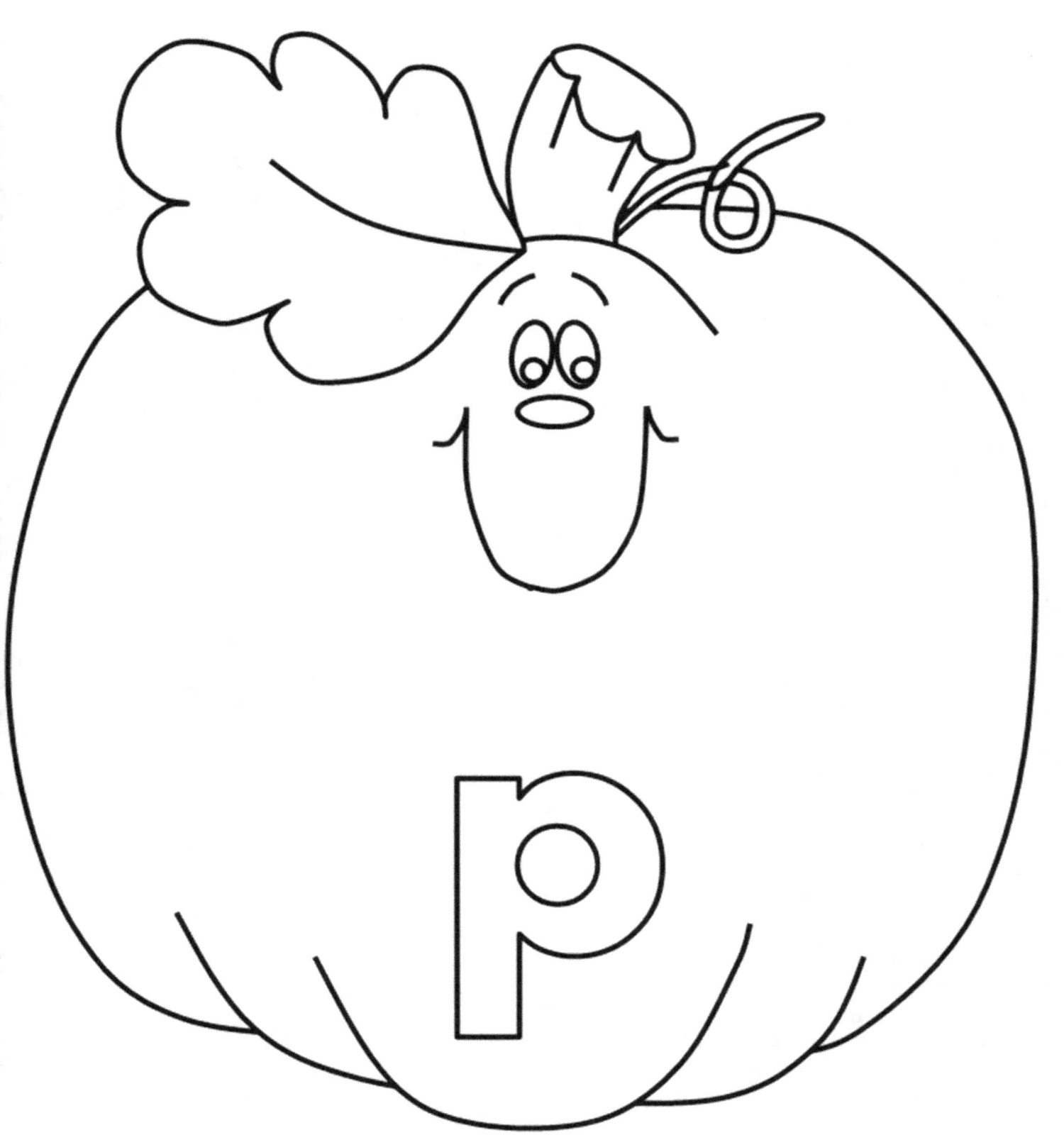

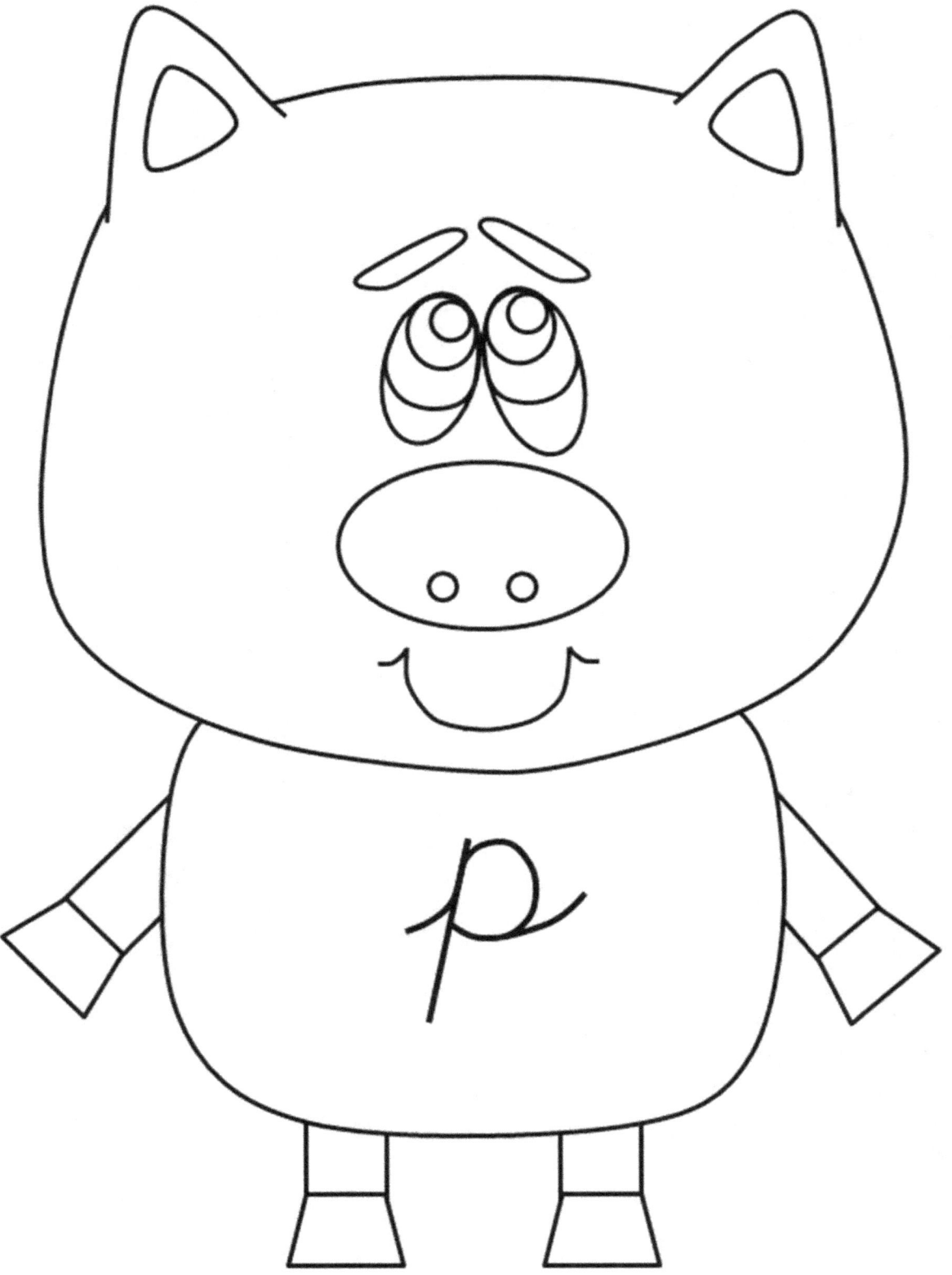

Trace the steps for making the letter p on the following line.

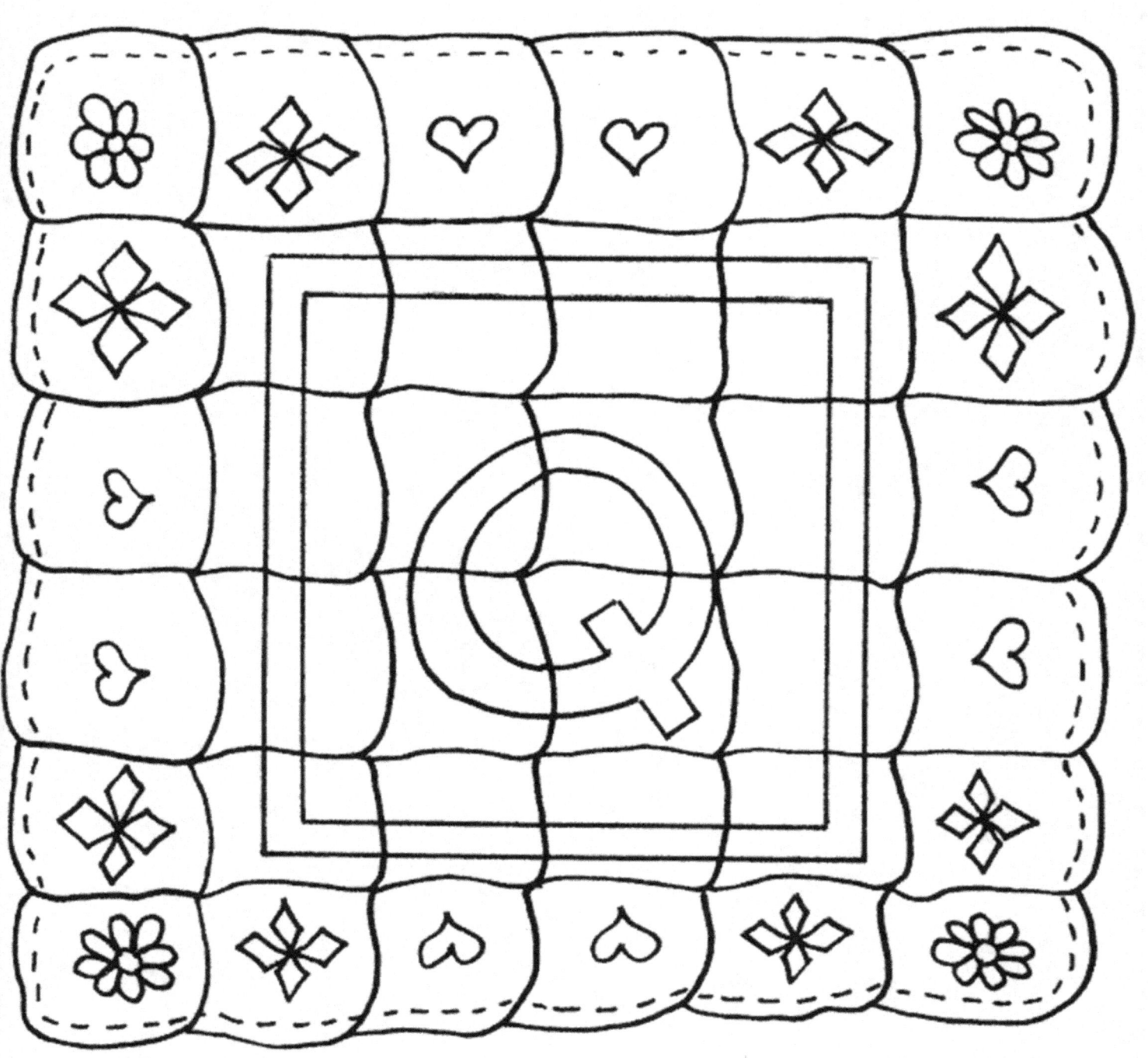

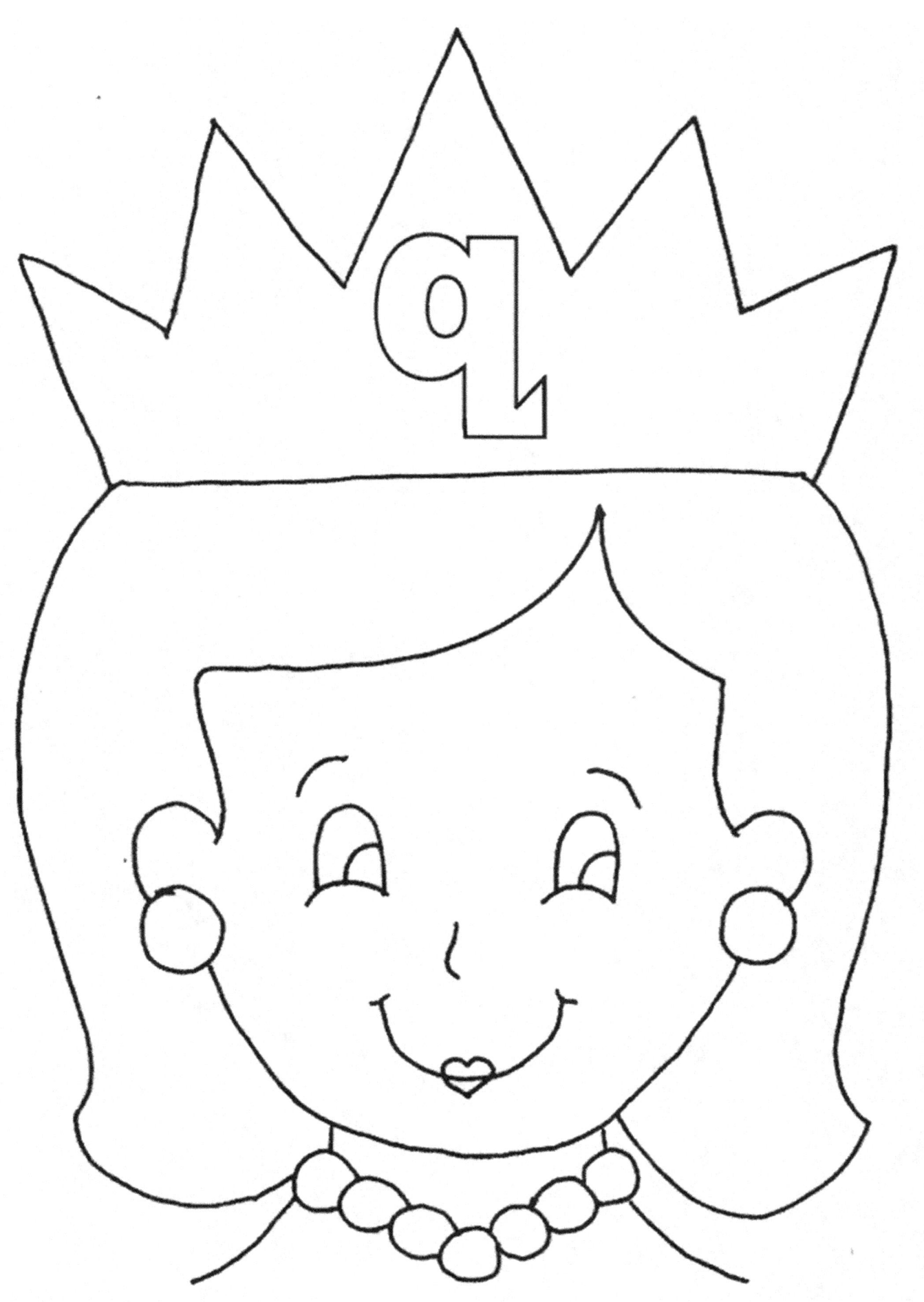

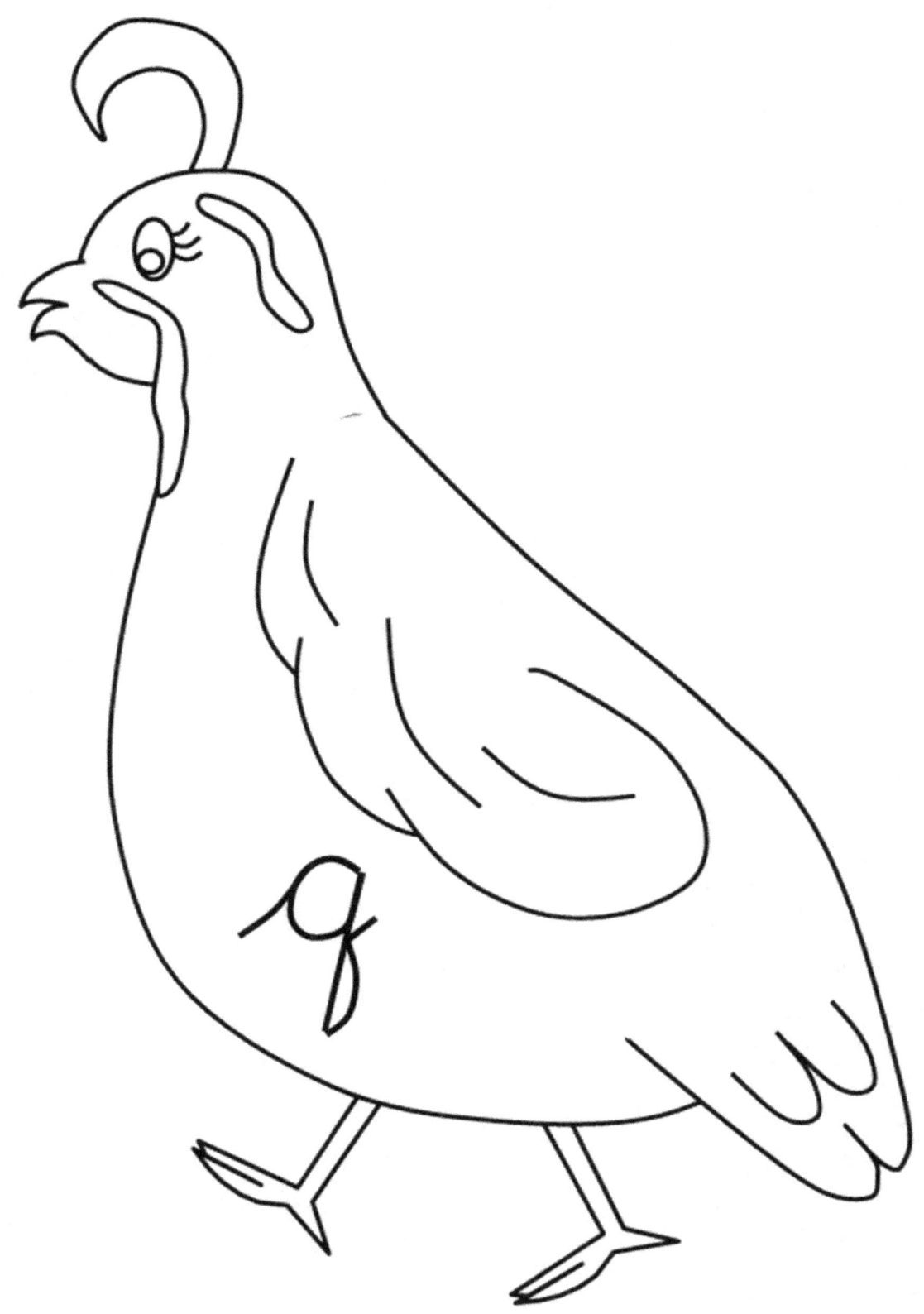

Trace the steps for making the letter q on the following line.

r c o q q q q

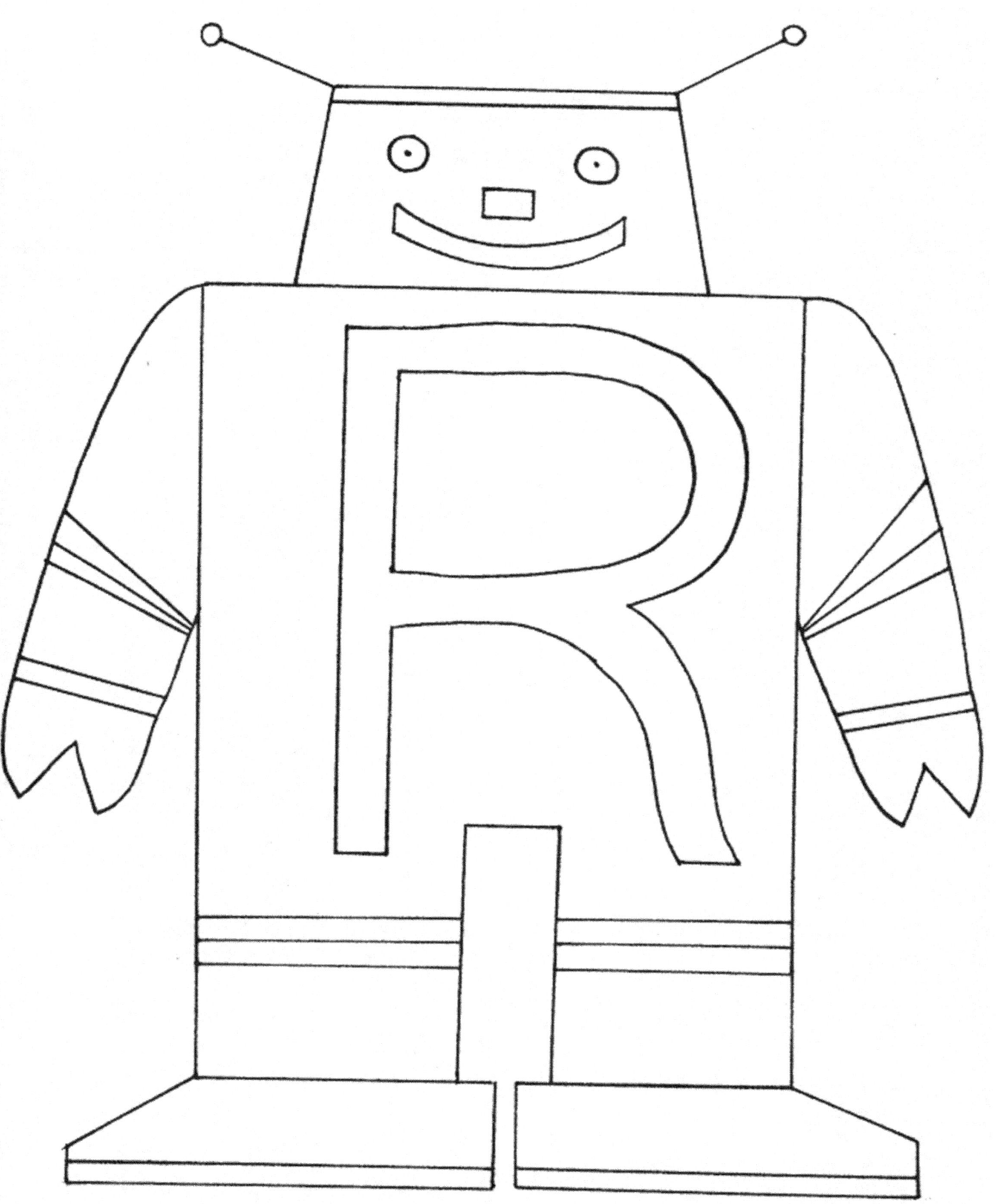

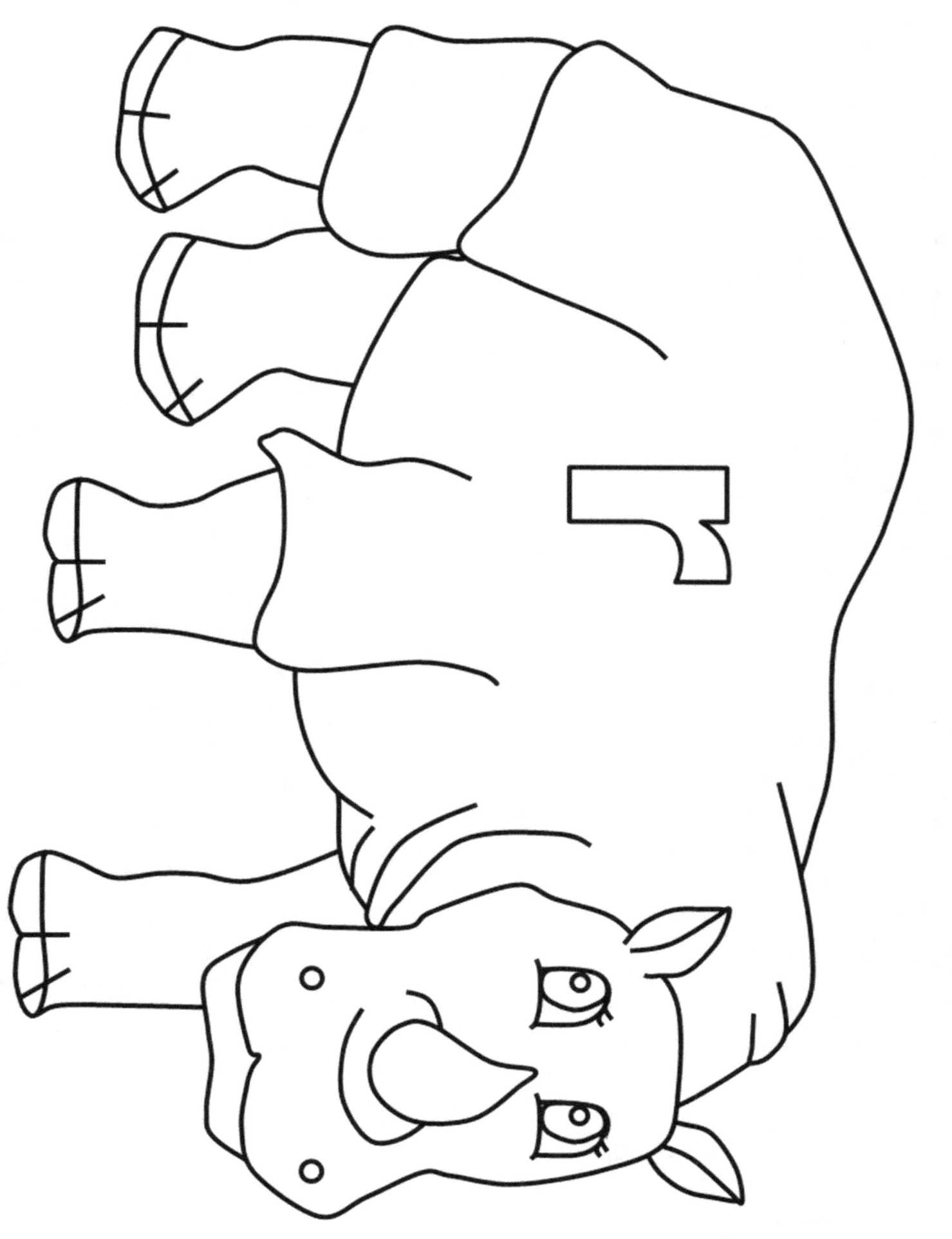

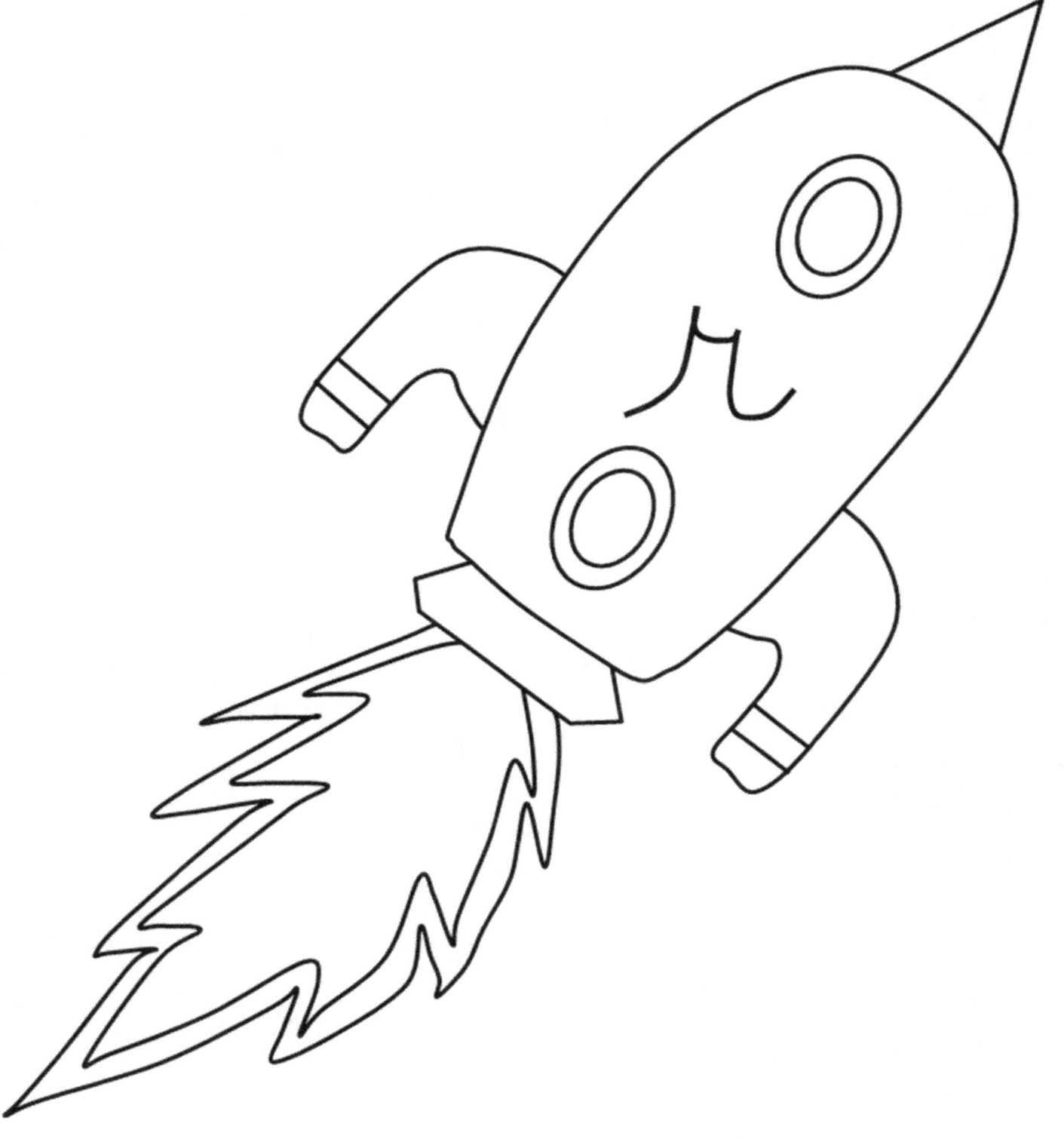

Trace the steps for making the letter r on the following line.

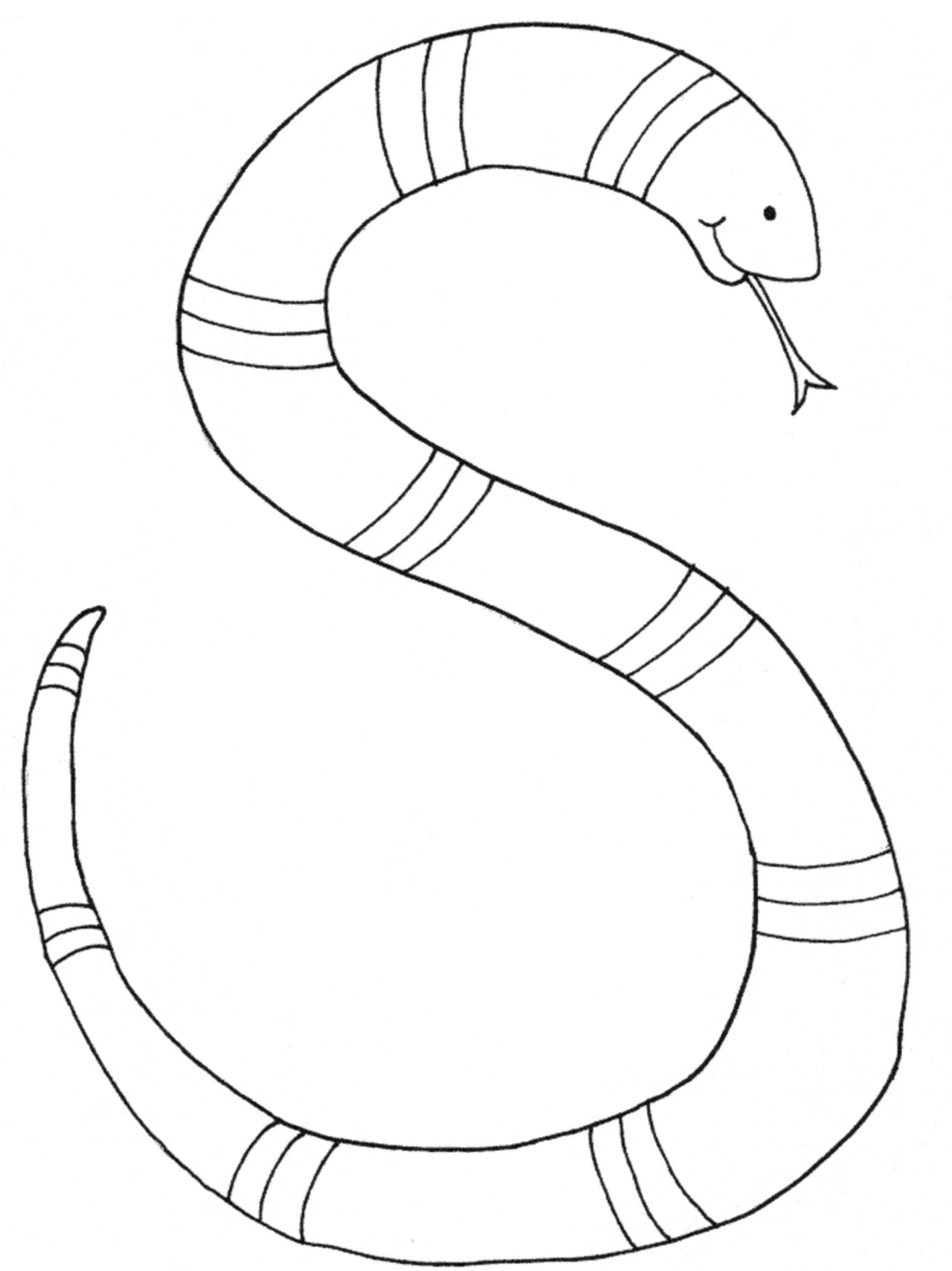

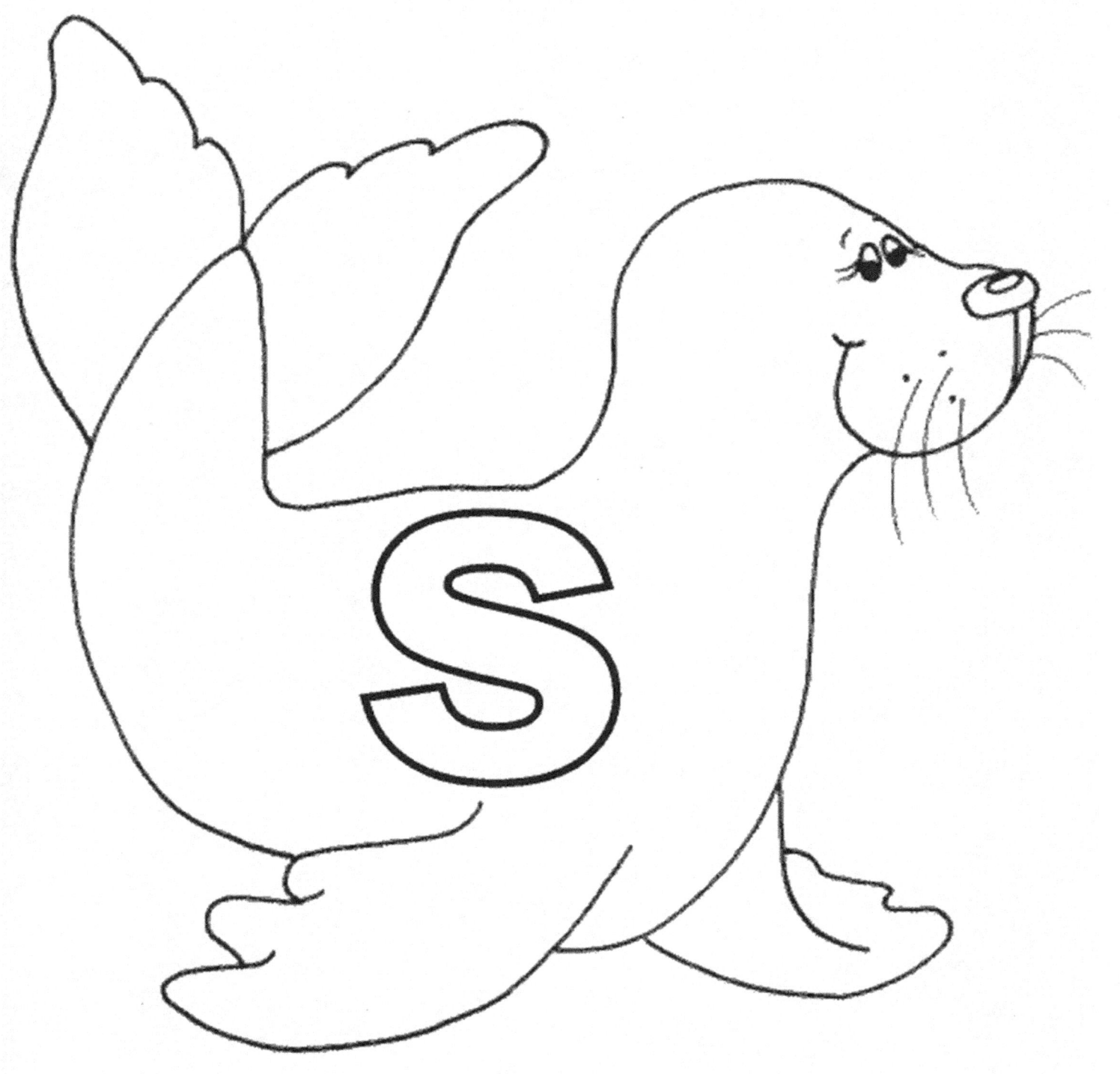

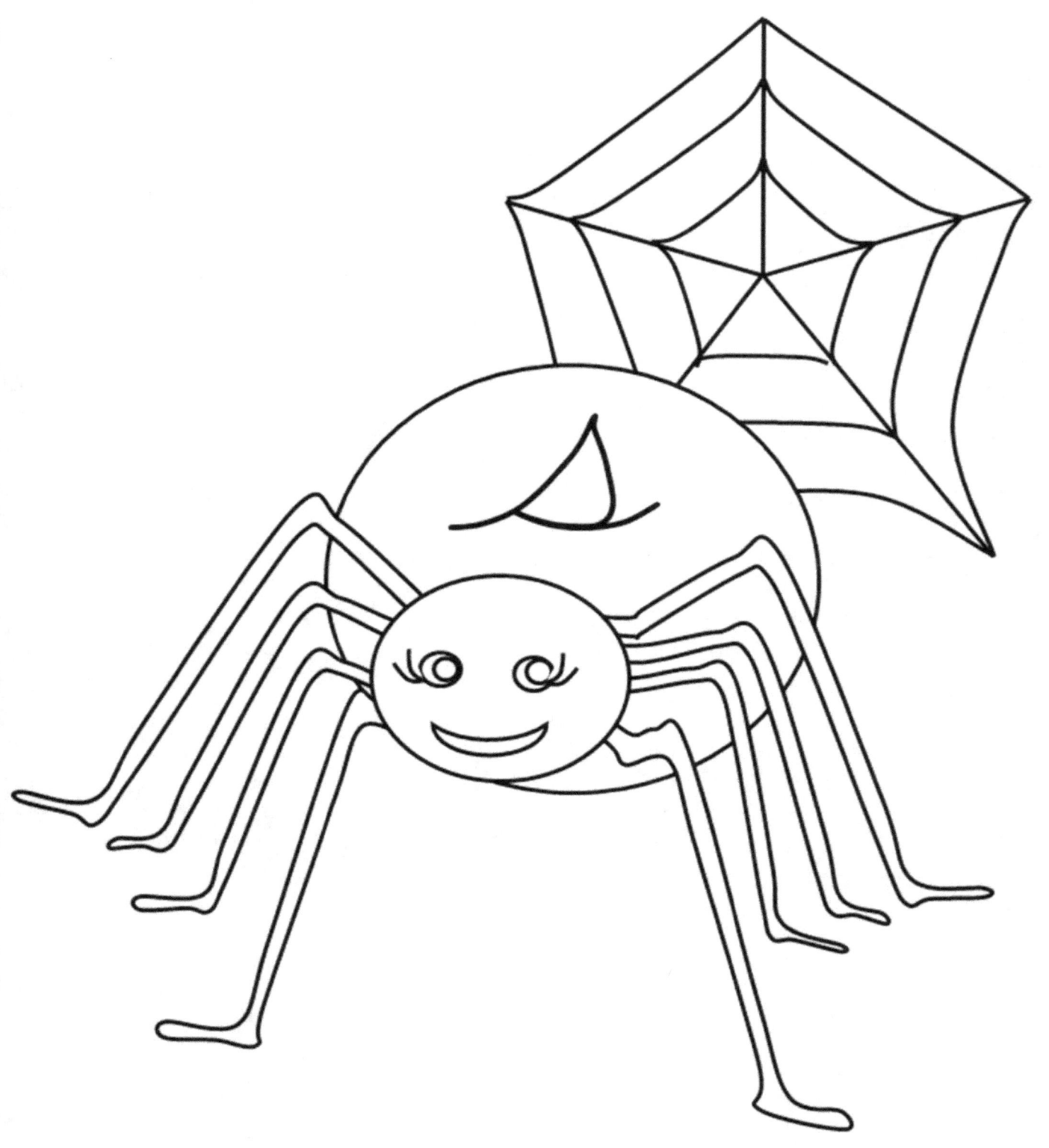

Trace the steps for making the letter s on the following line.

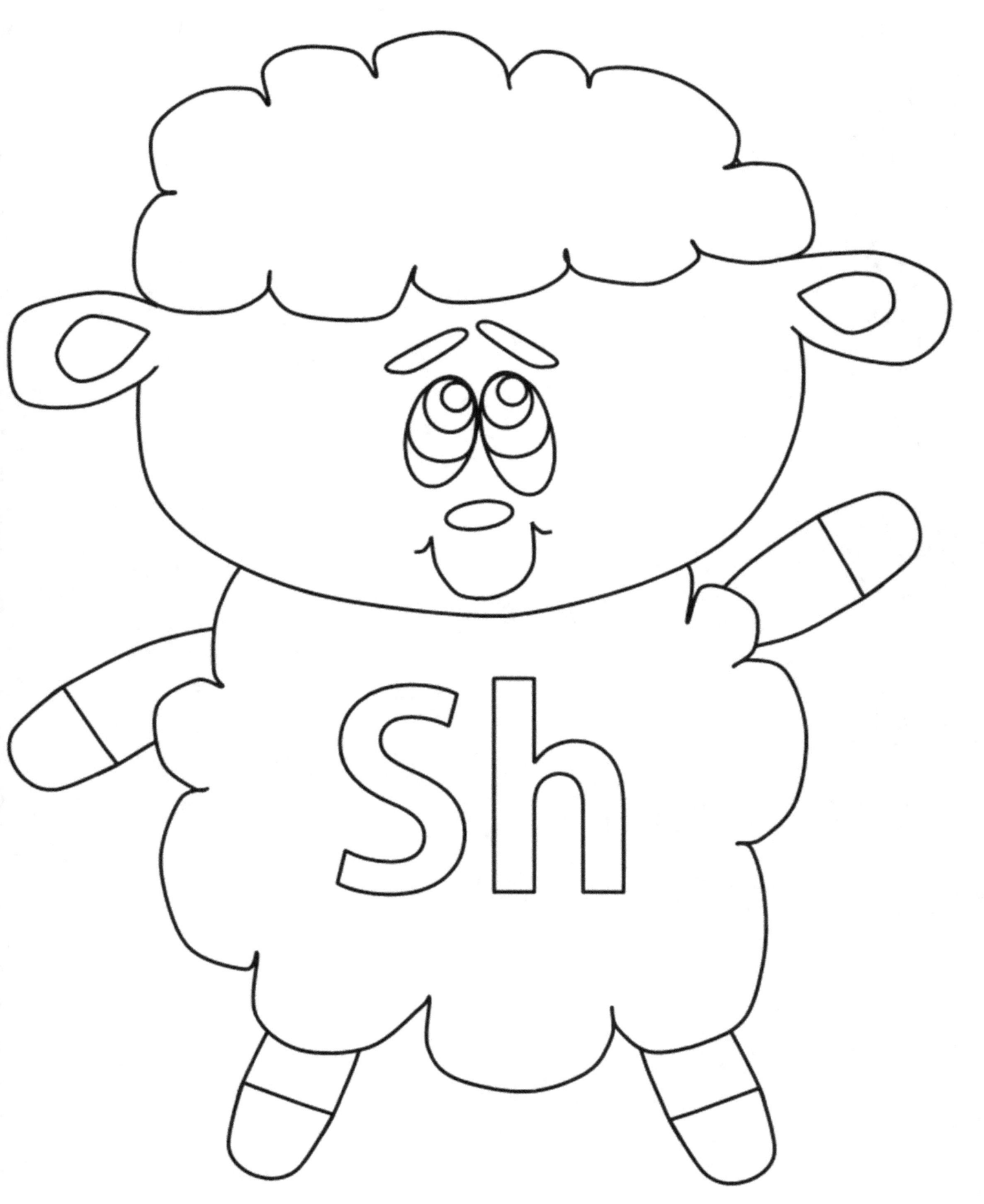

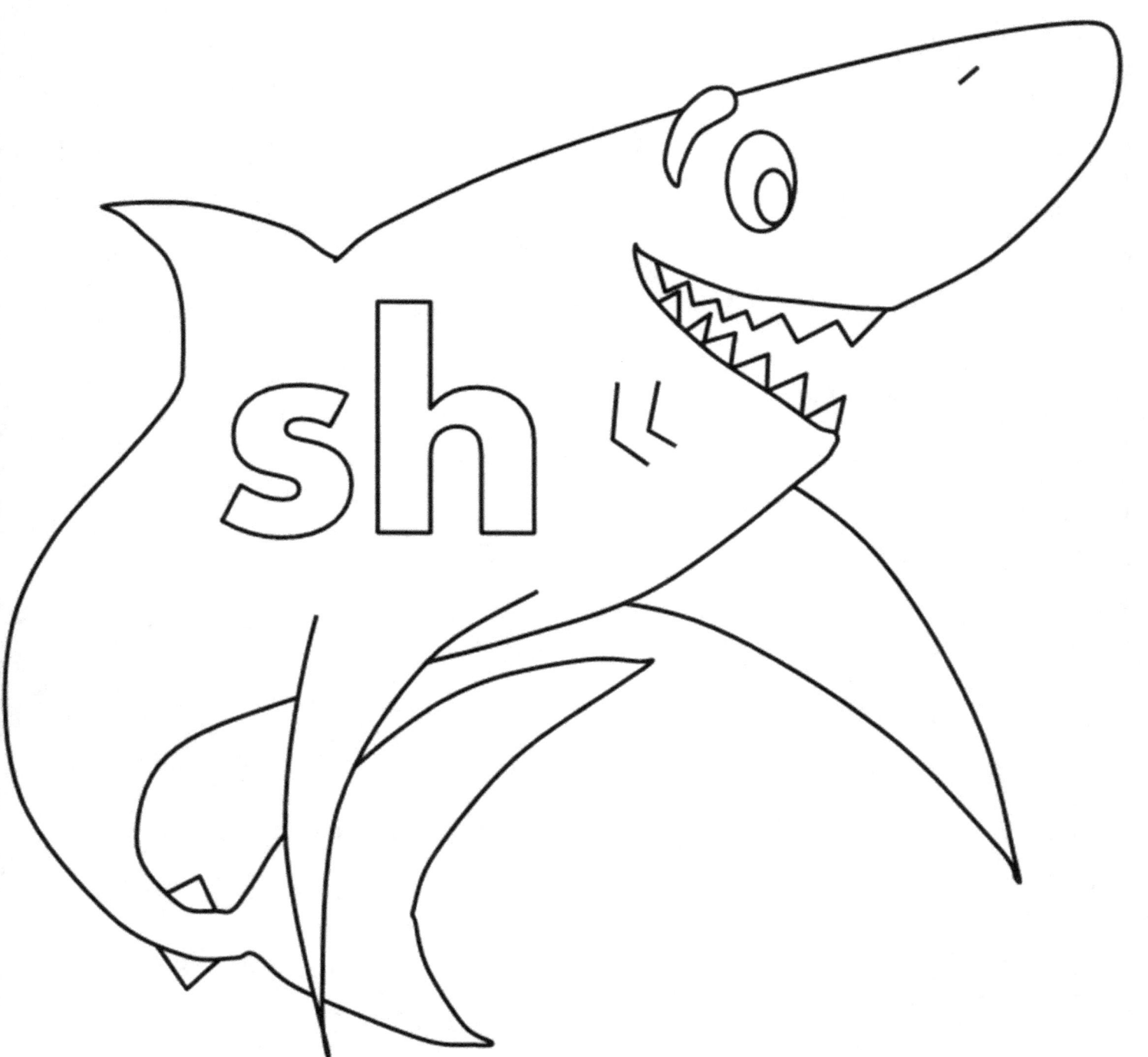

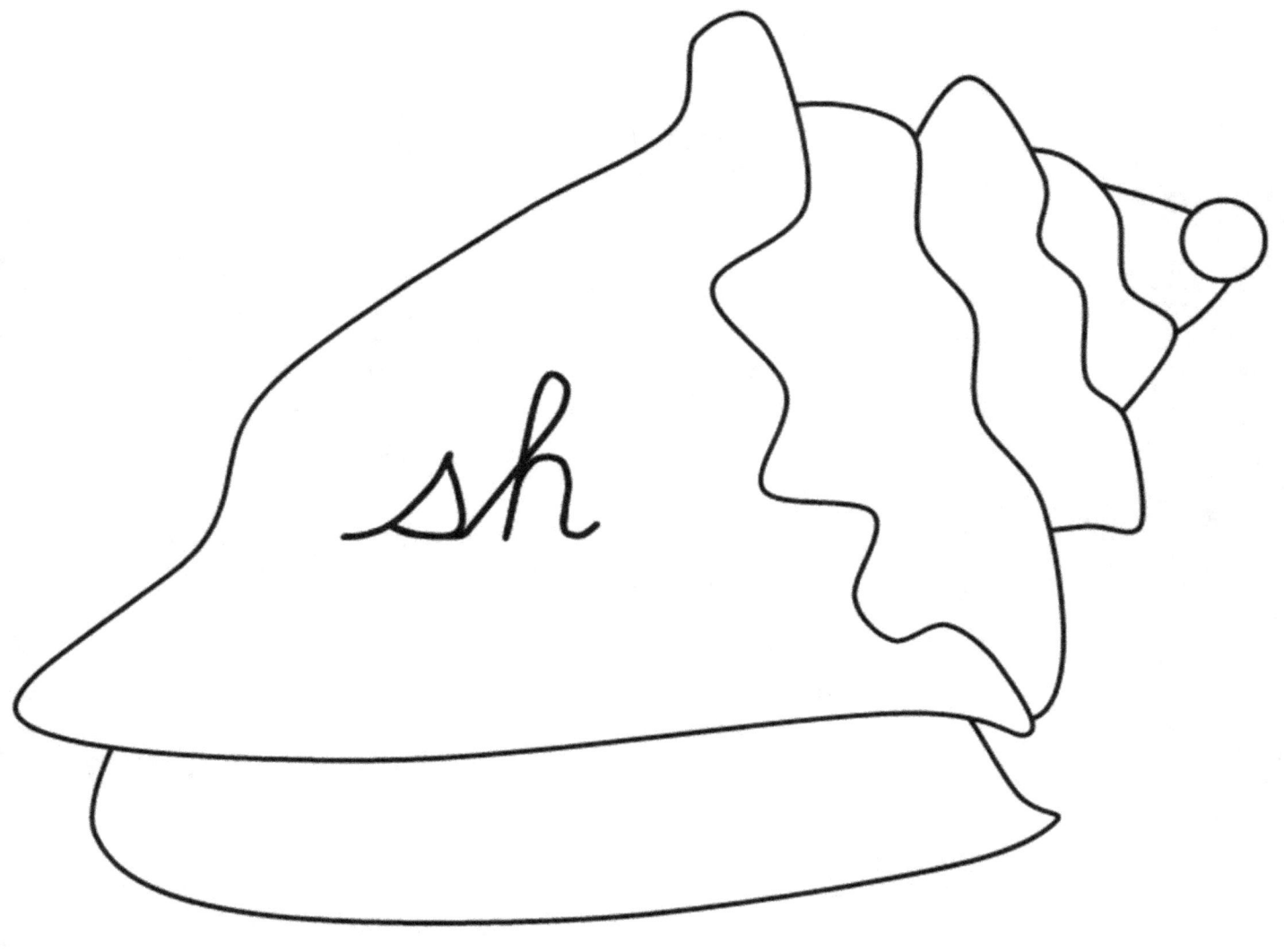

Trace the steps for making the letter sh on the following line.

s   h   sh   sh   sh   sh

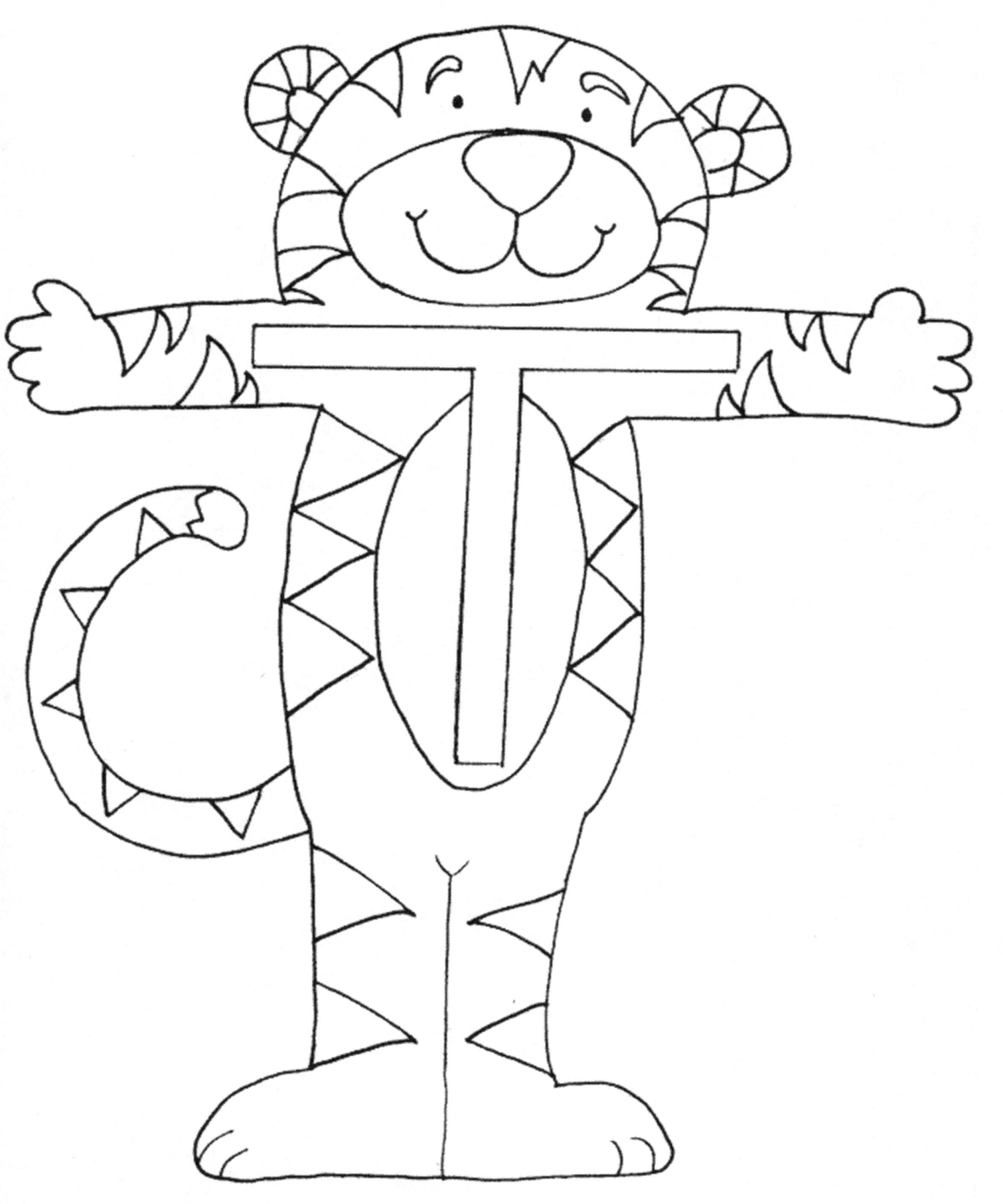

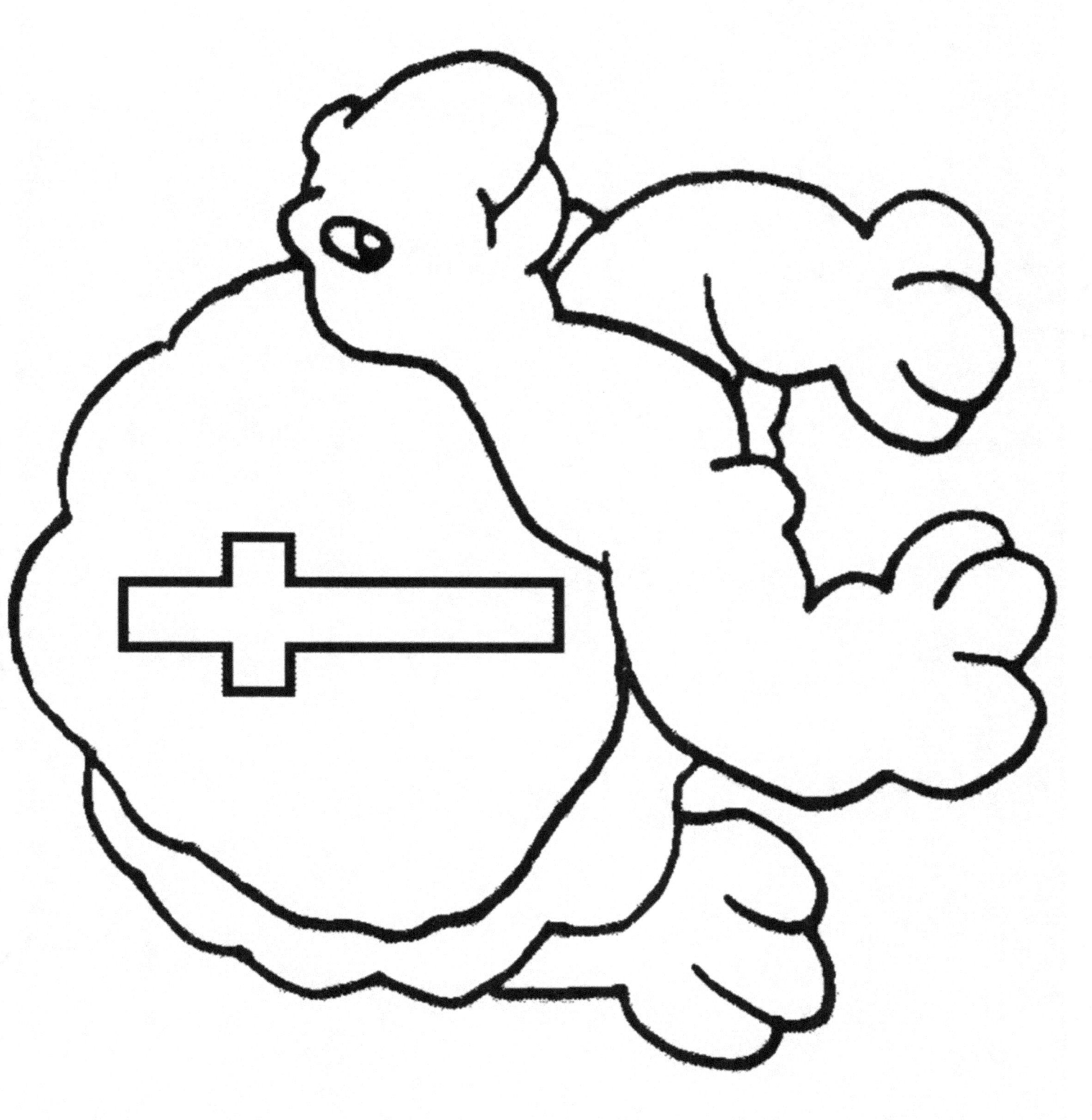

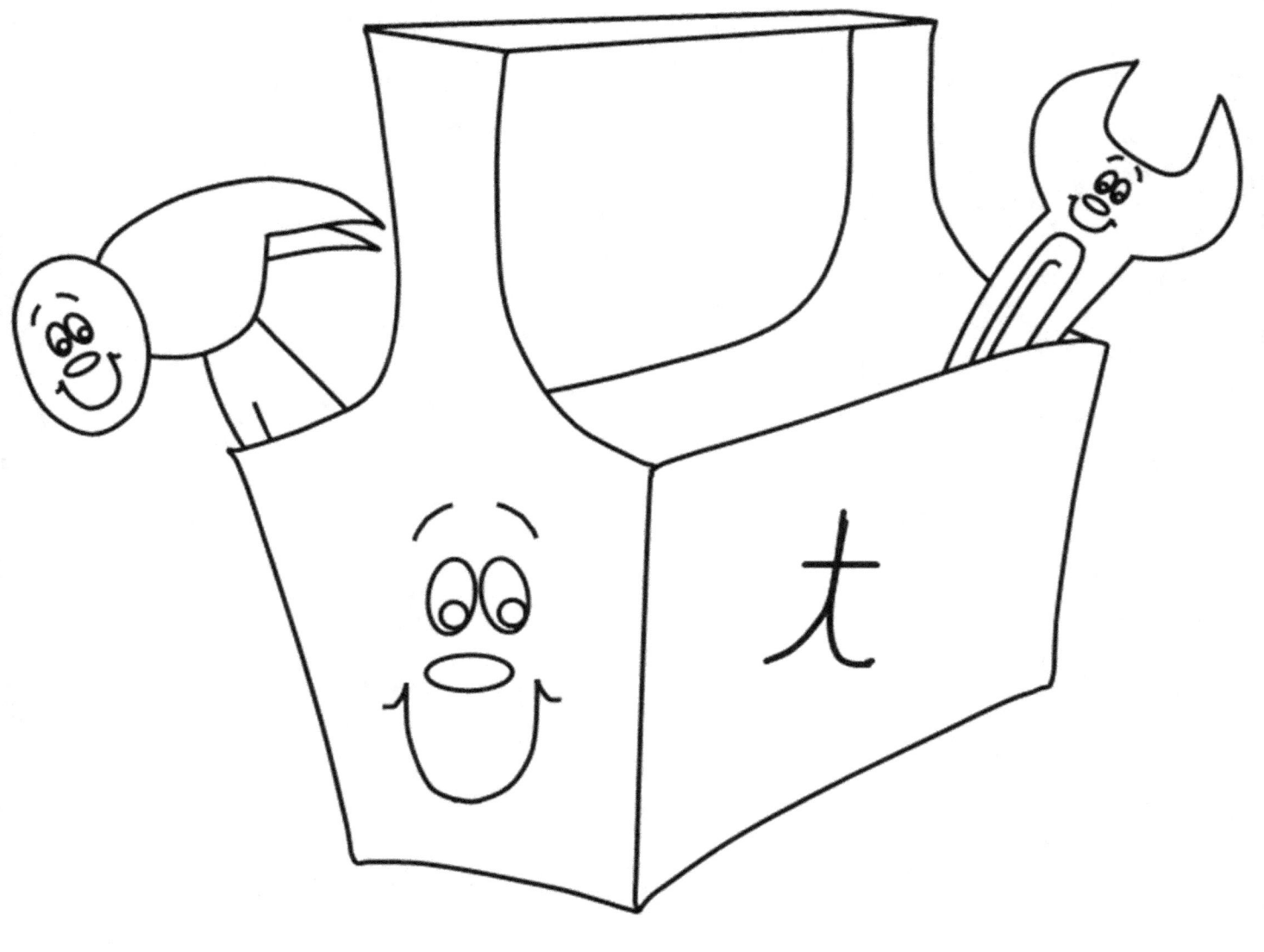

Trace the steps for making the letter t on the following line.

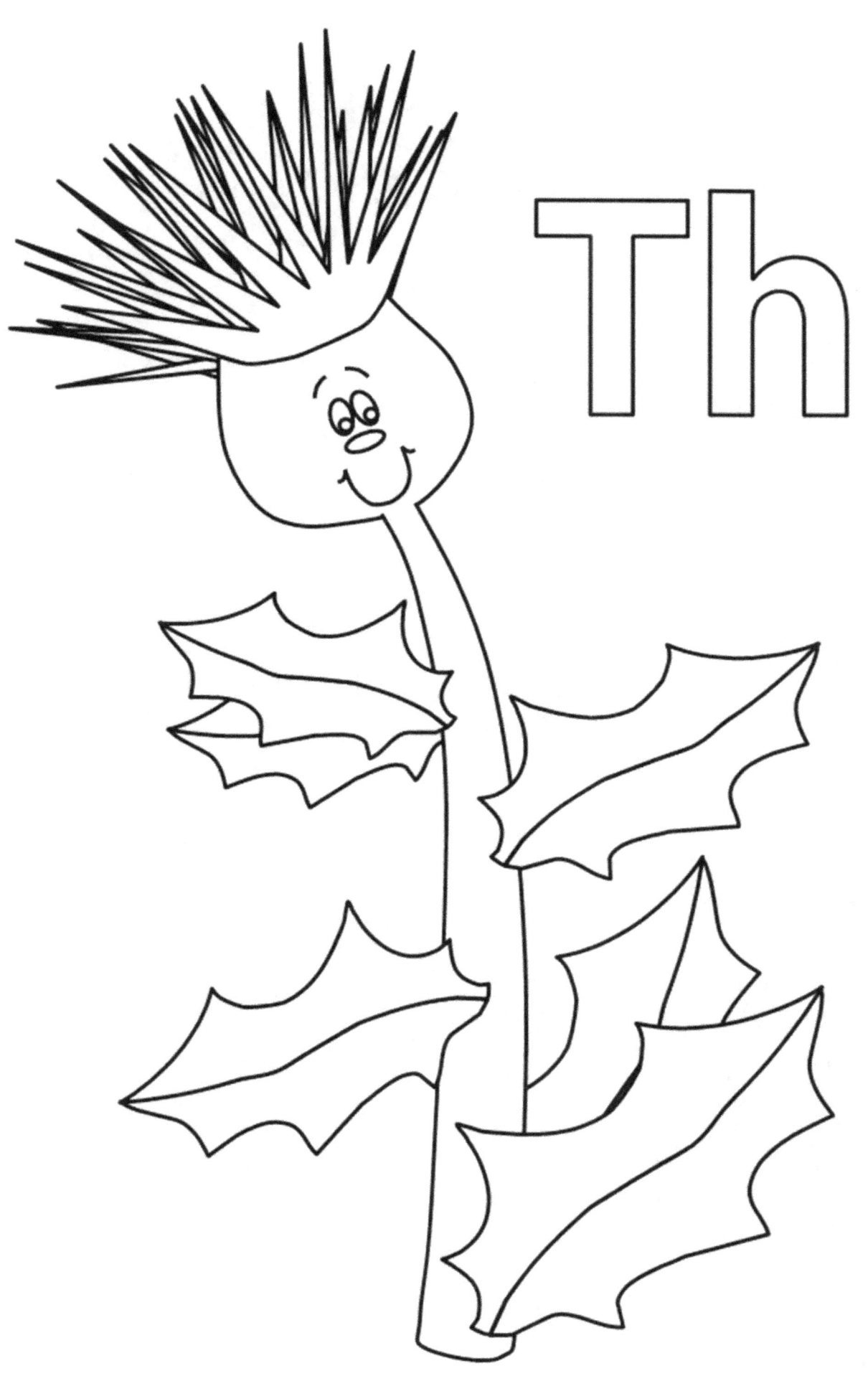

Th

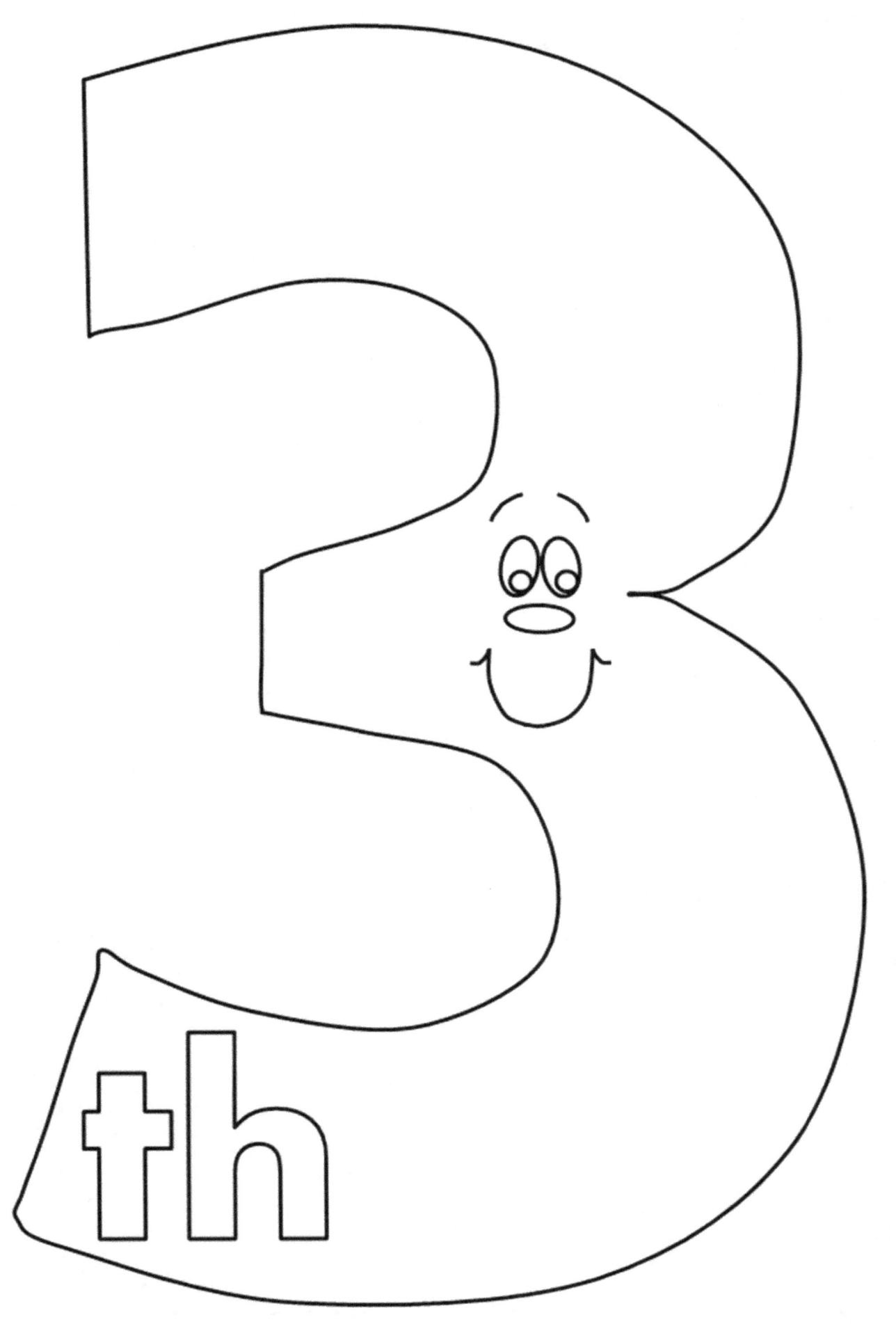

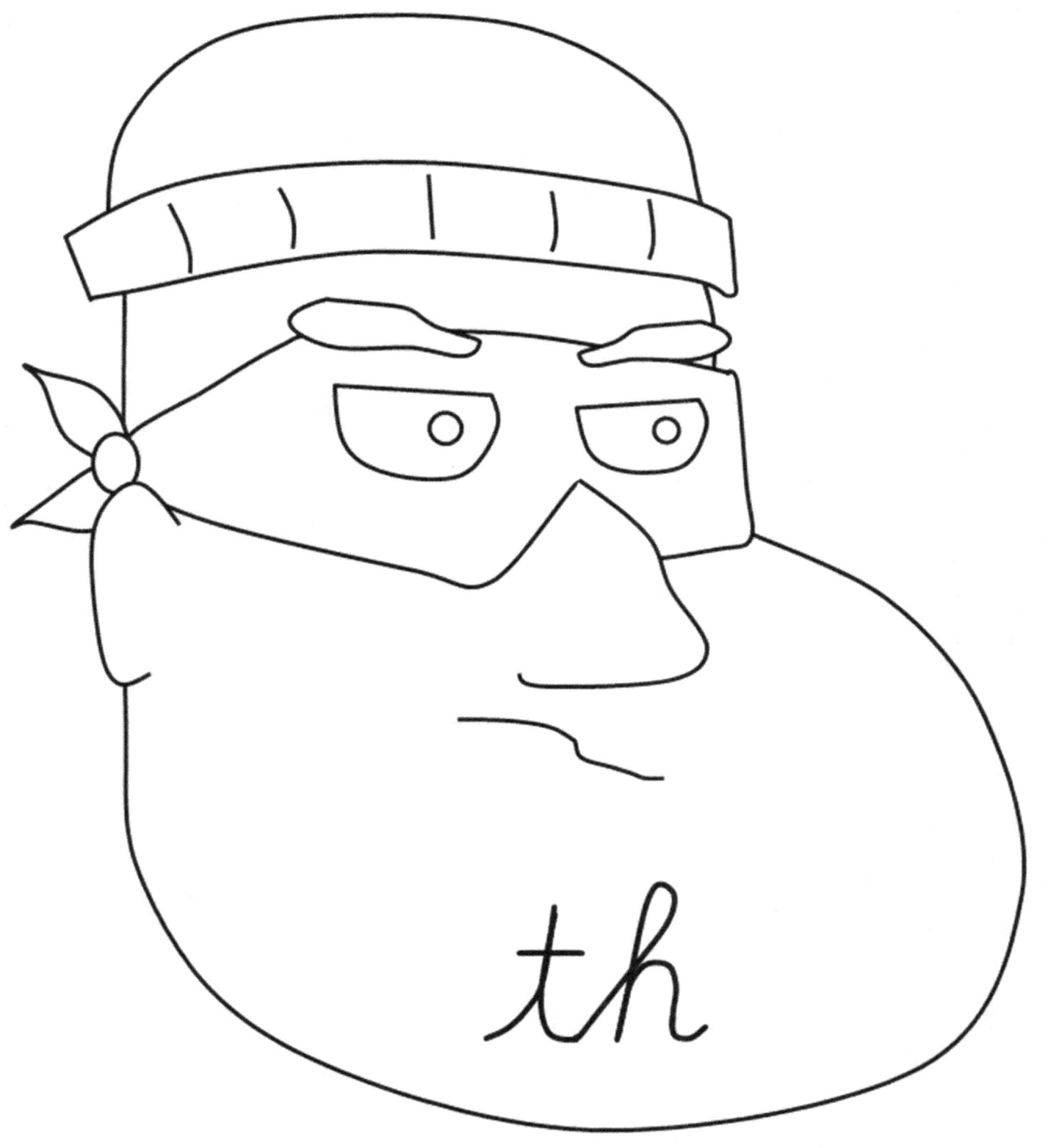

Trace the steps for making the letter th on the following line.

t -- *h* -- *th* -- *th* -- *th* -- *th*

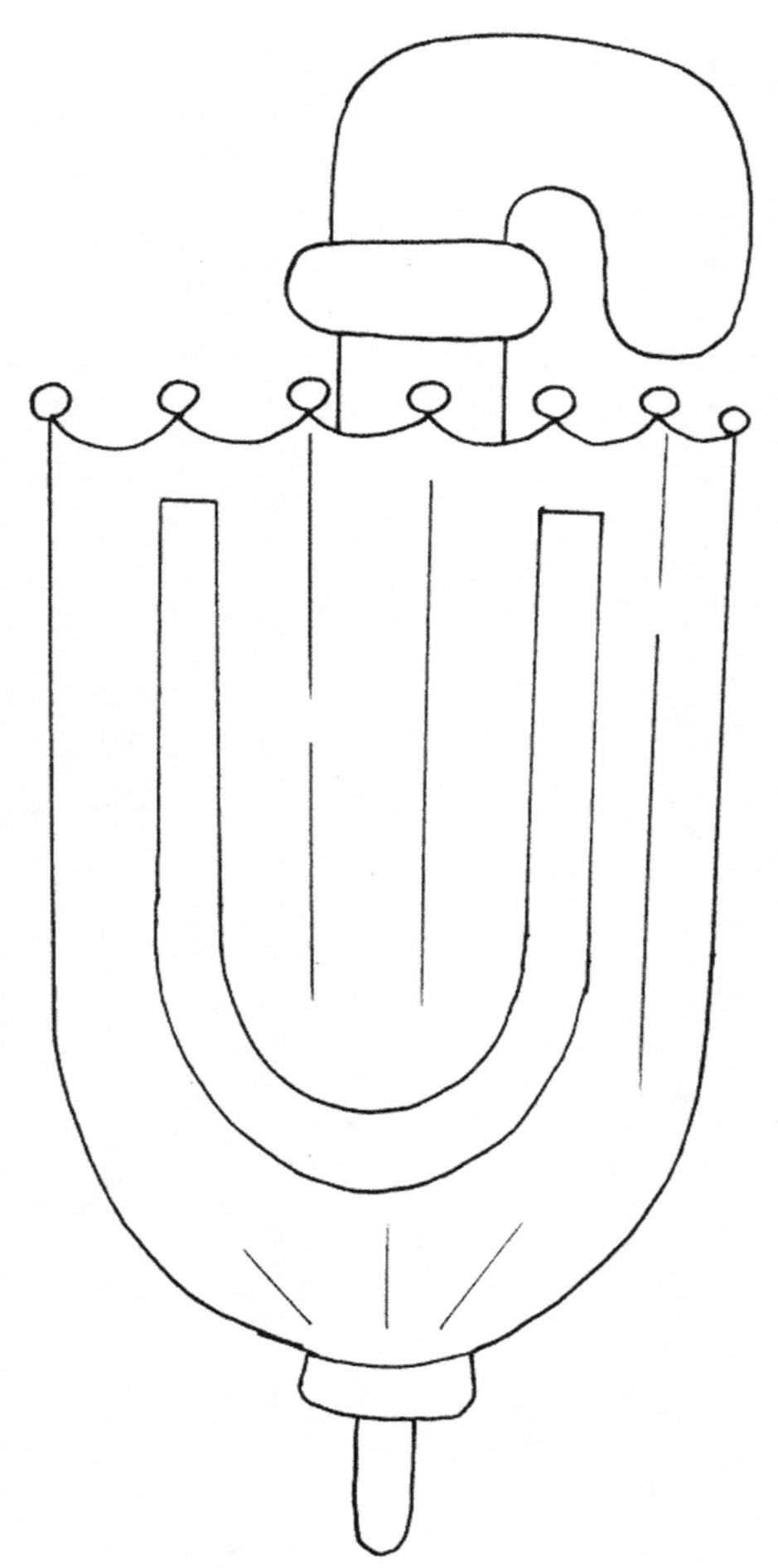

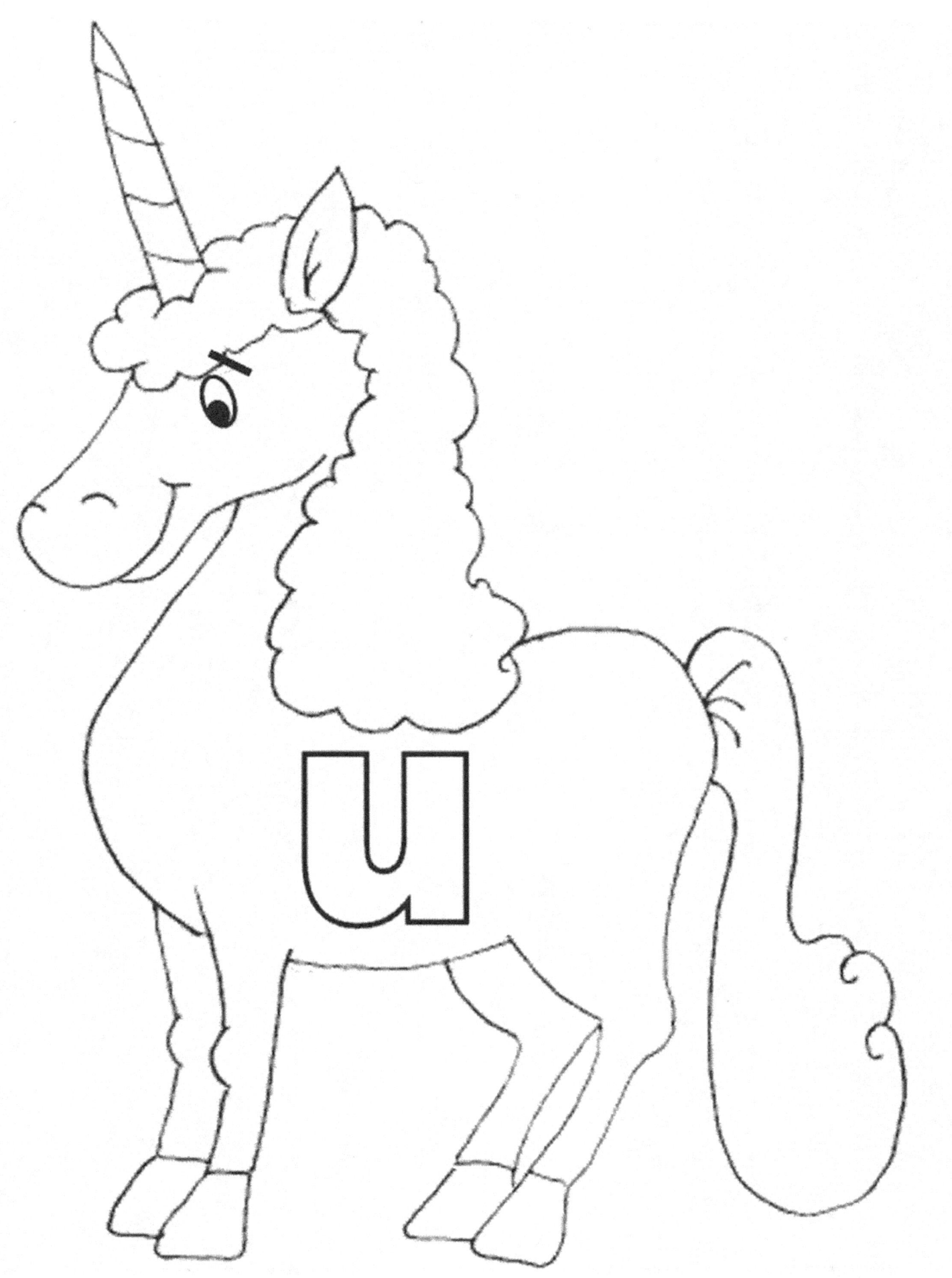

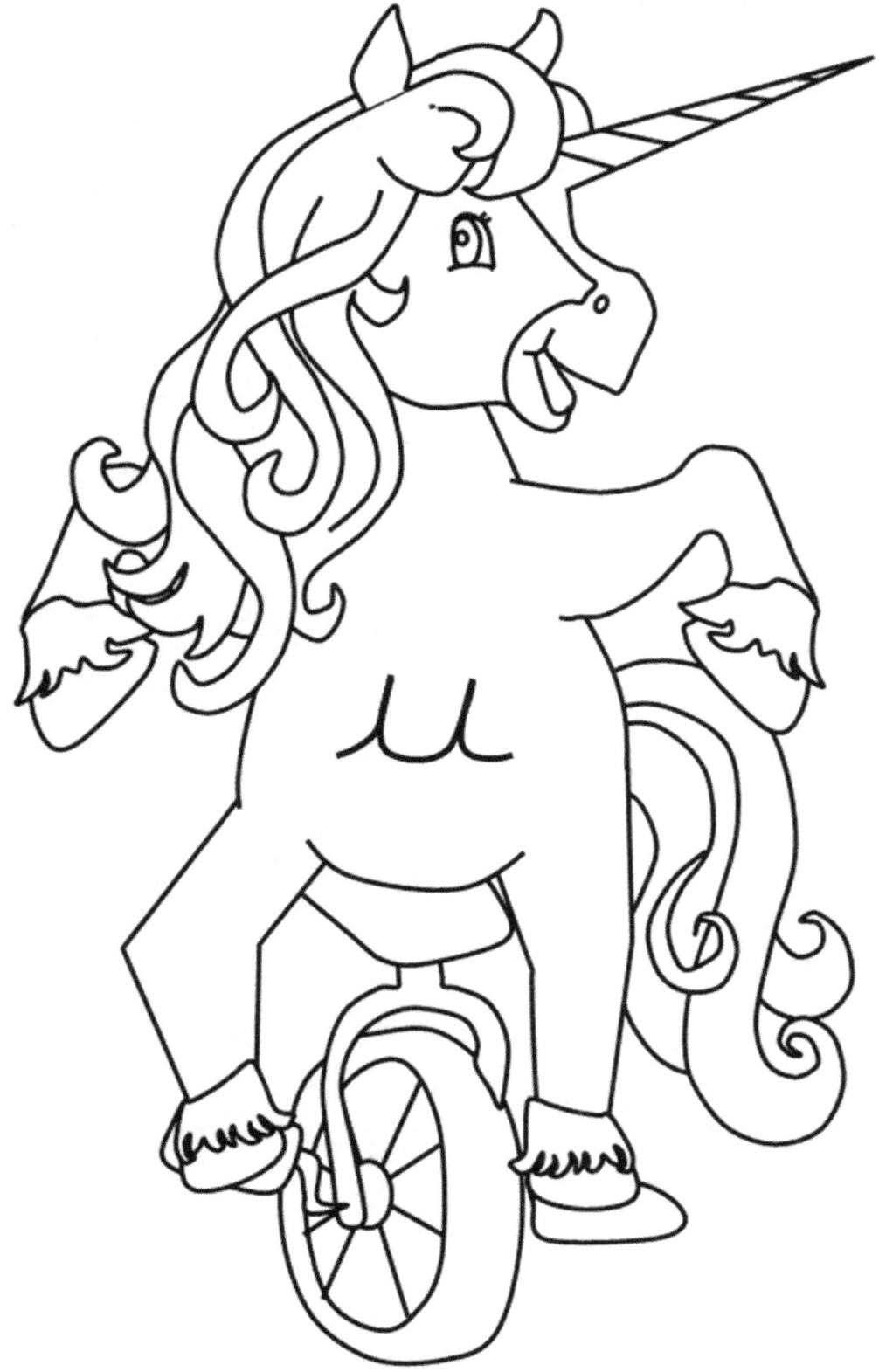

Trace the steps for making the letter u on the following line.

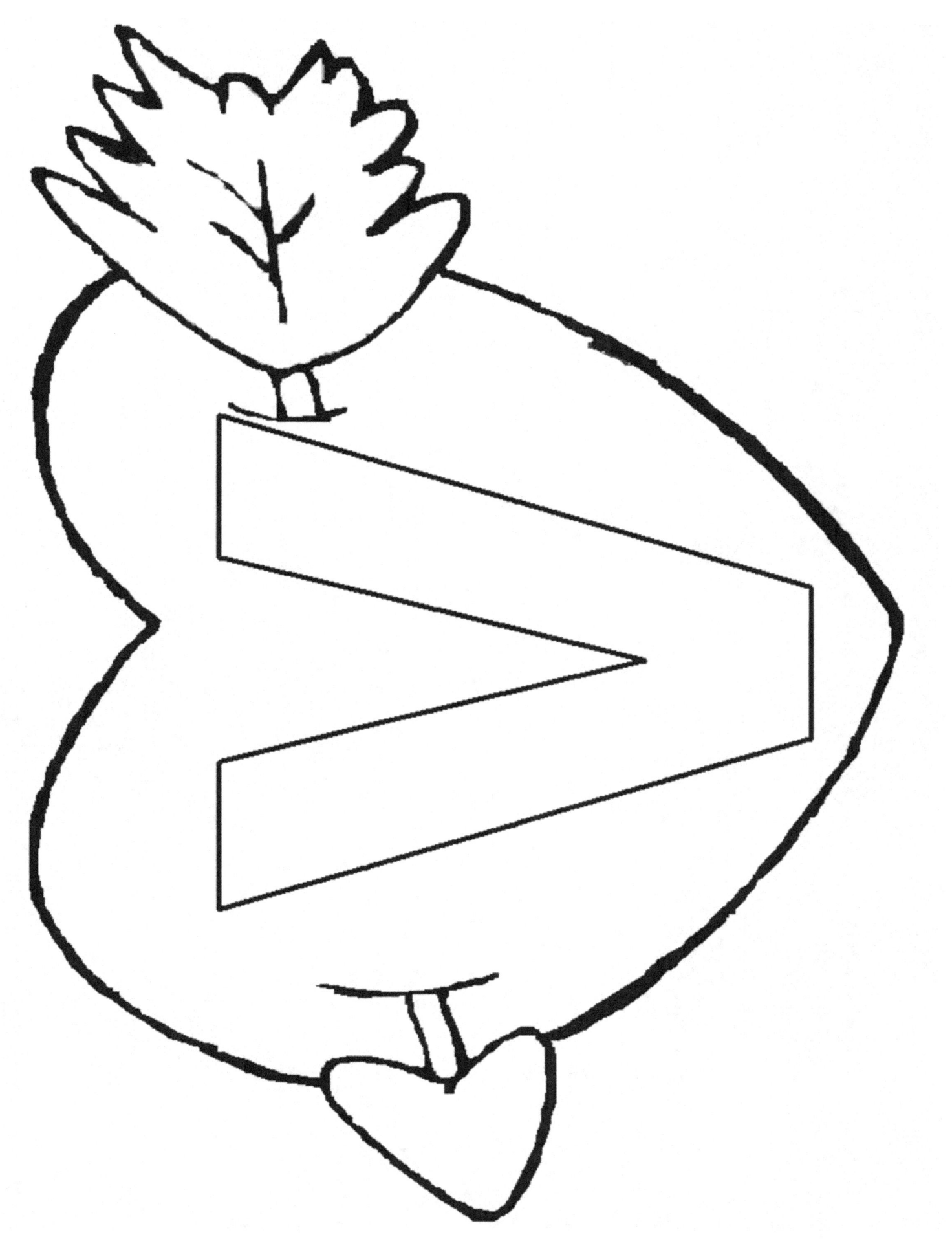

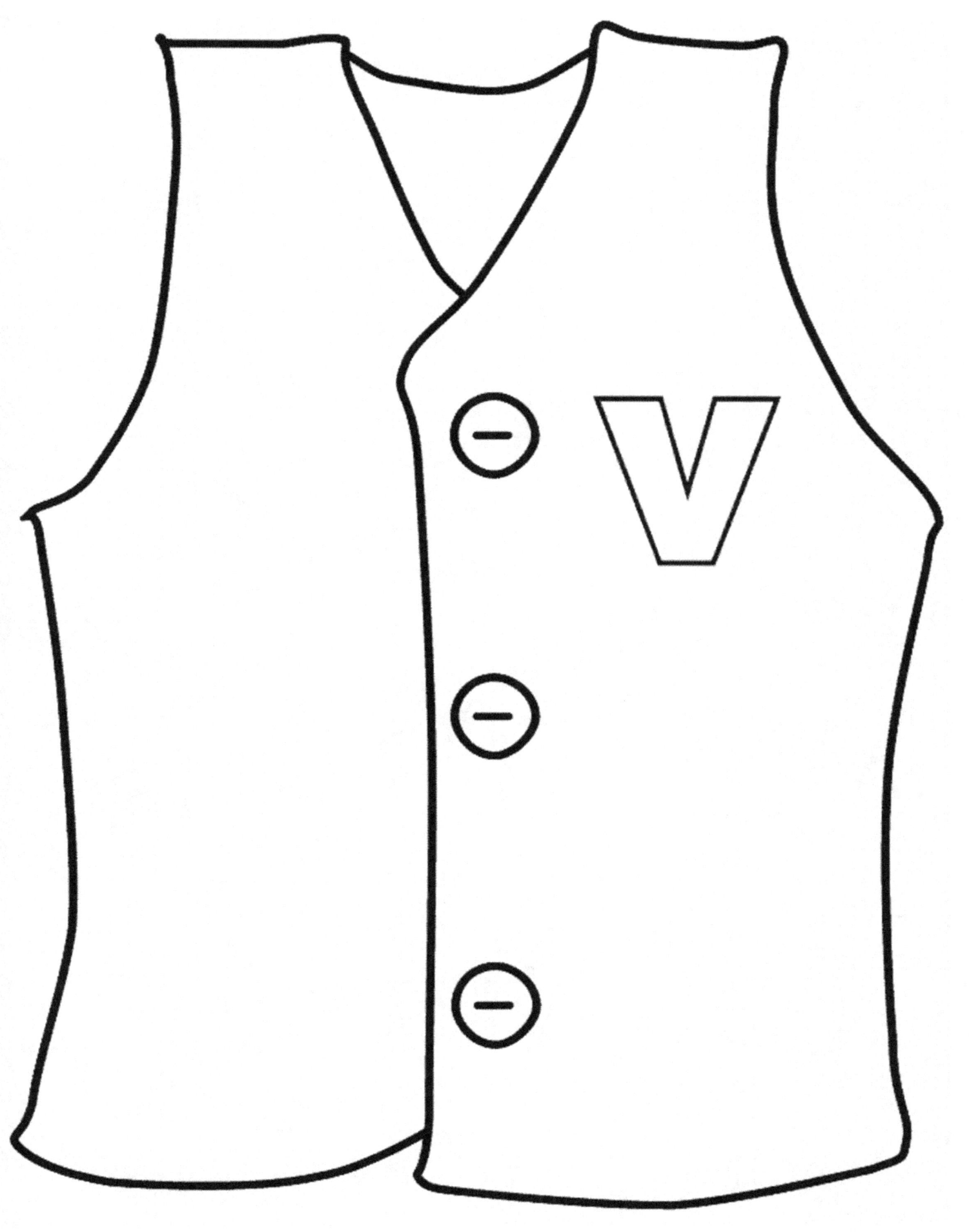

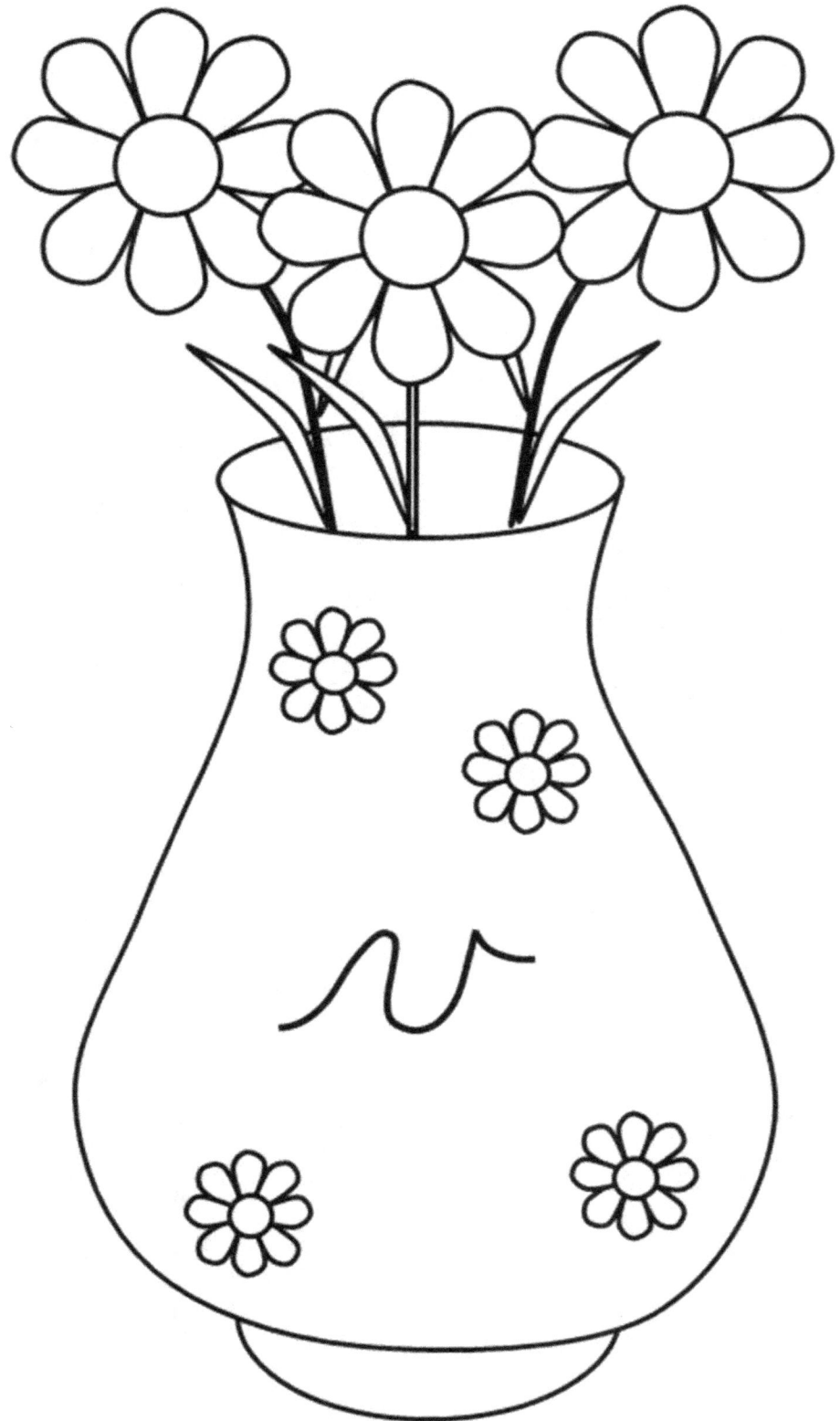

Trace the steps for making the letter v on the following line.

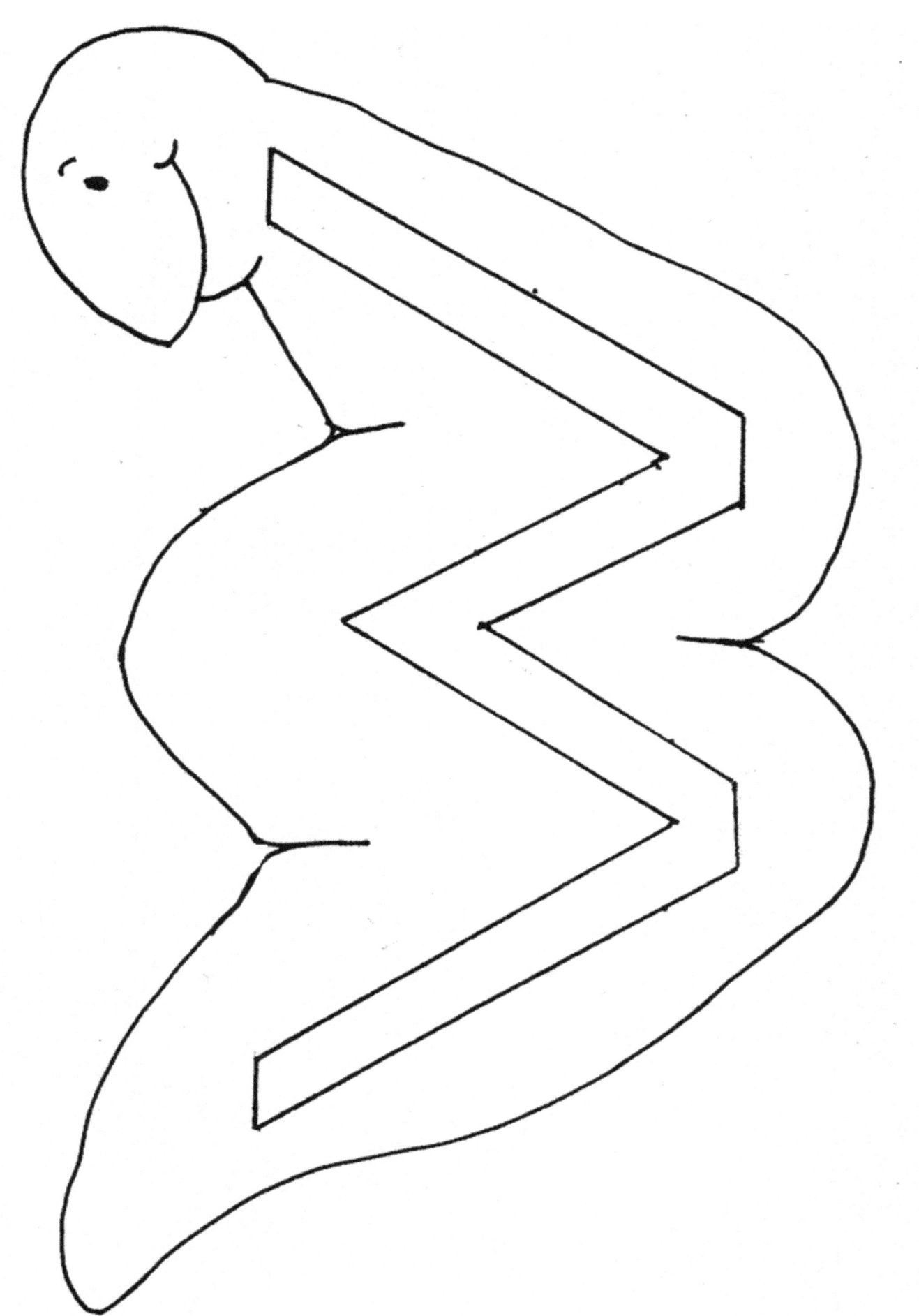

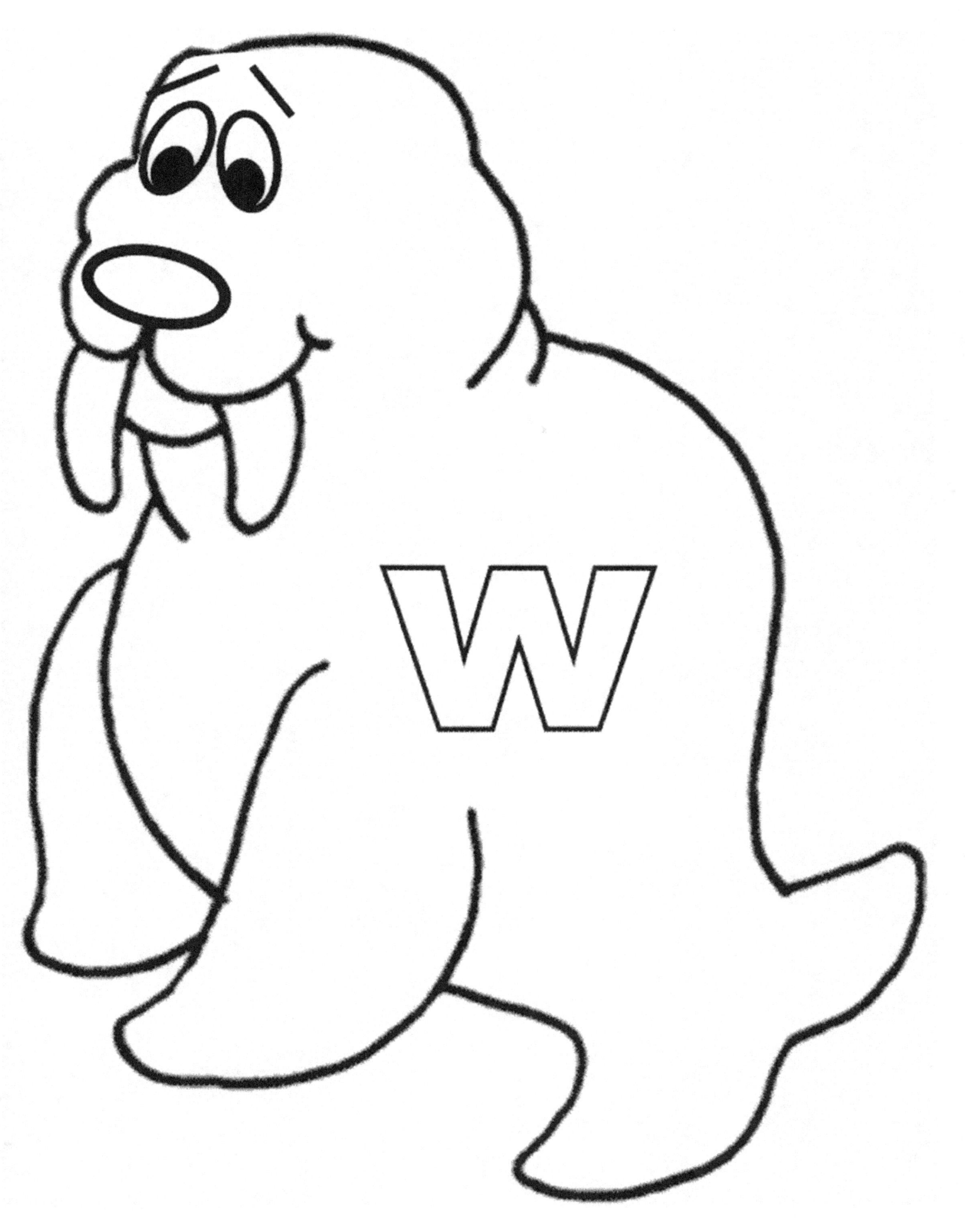

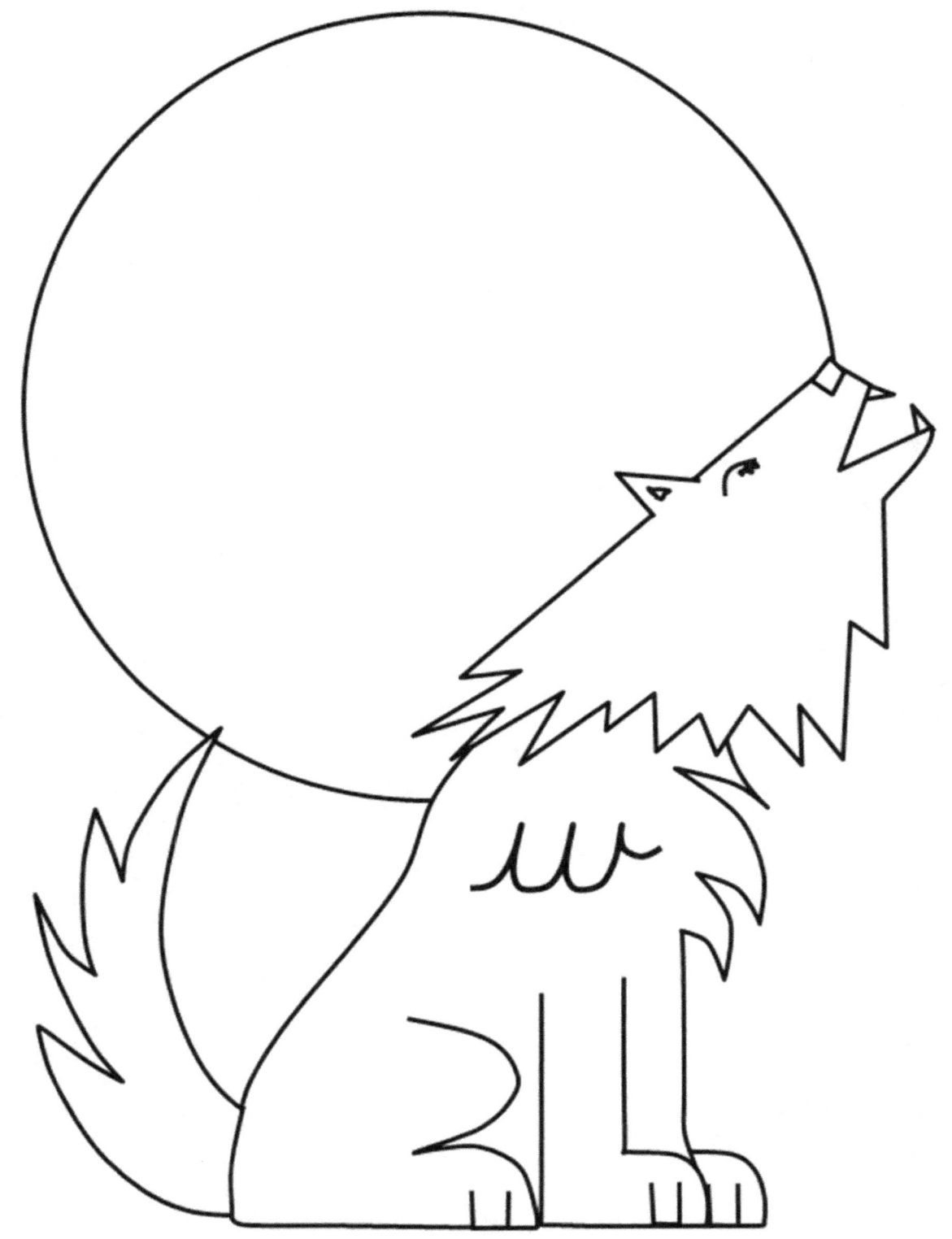

Trace the steps for making the letter w on the following line.

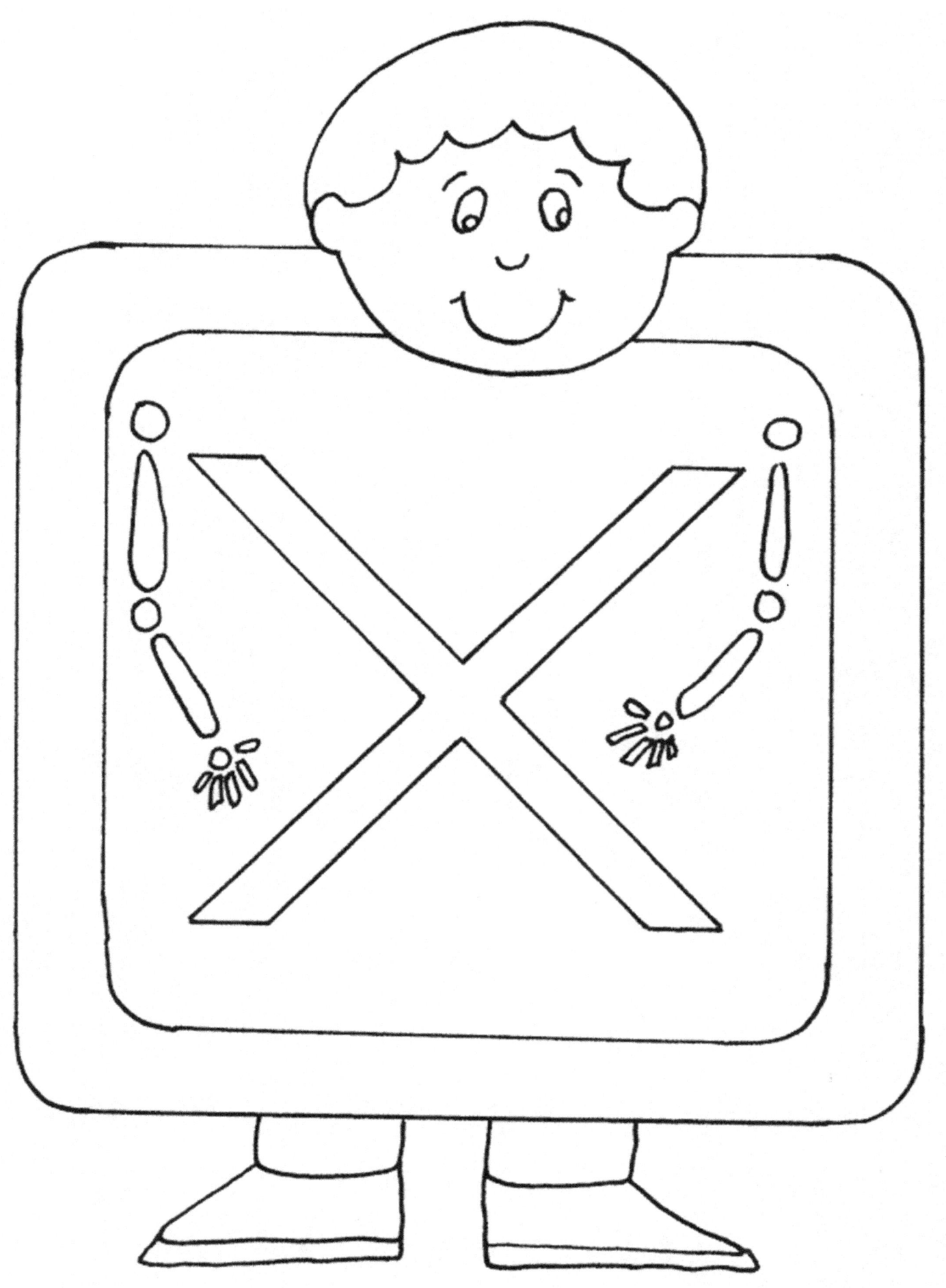

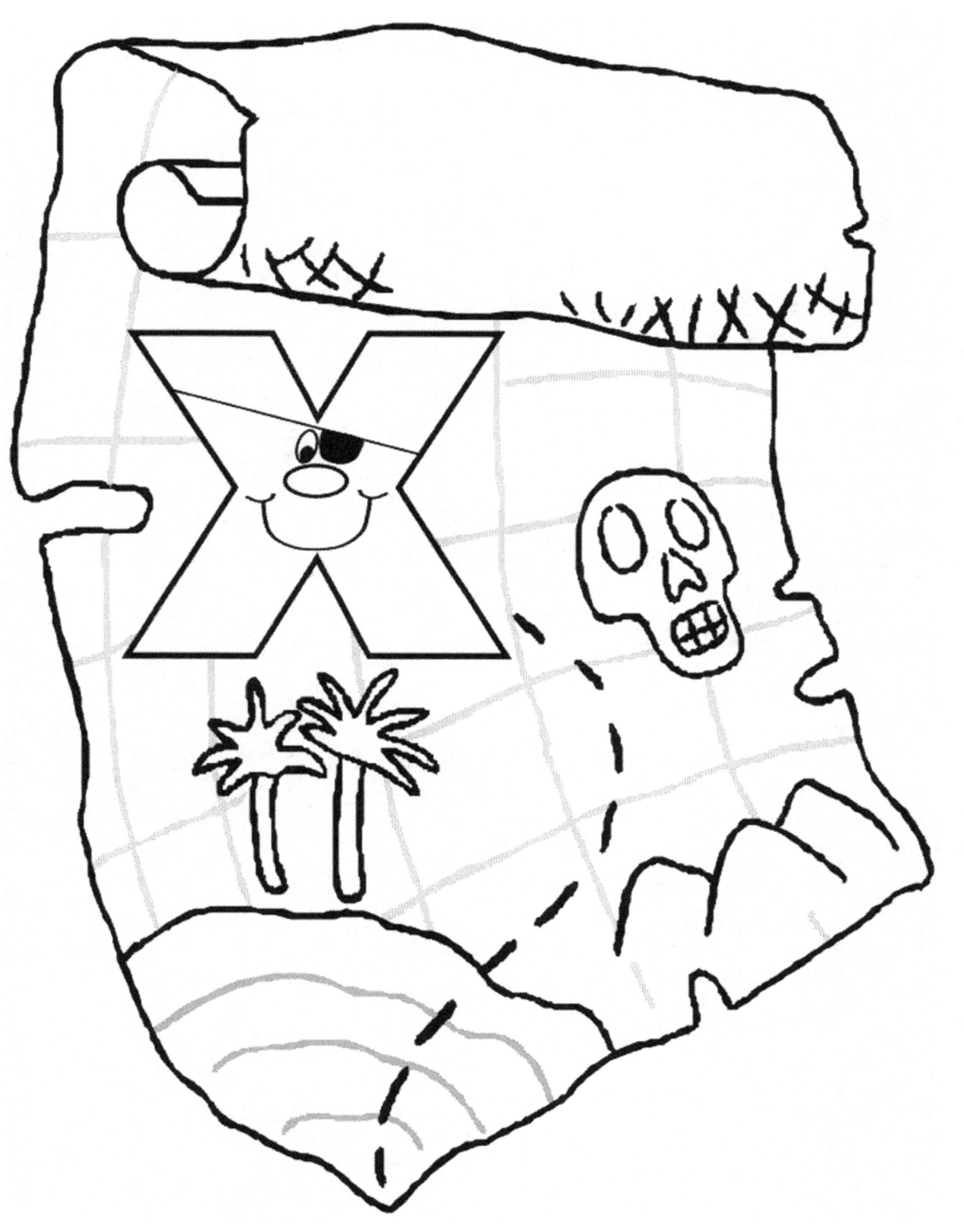

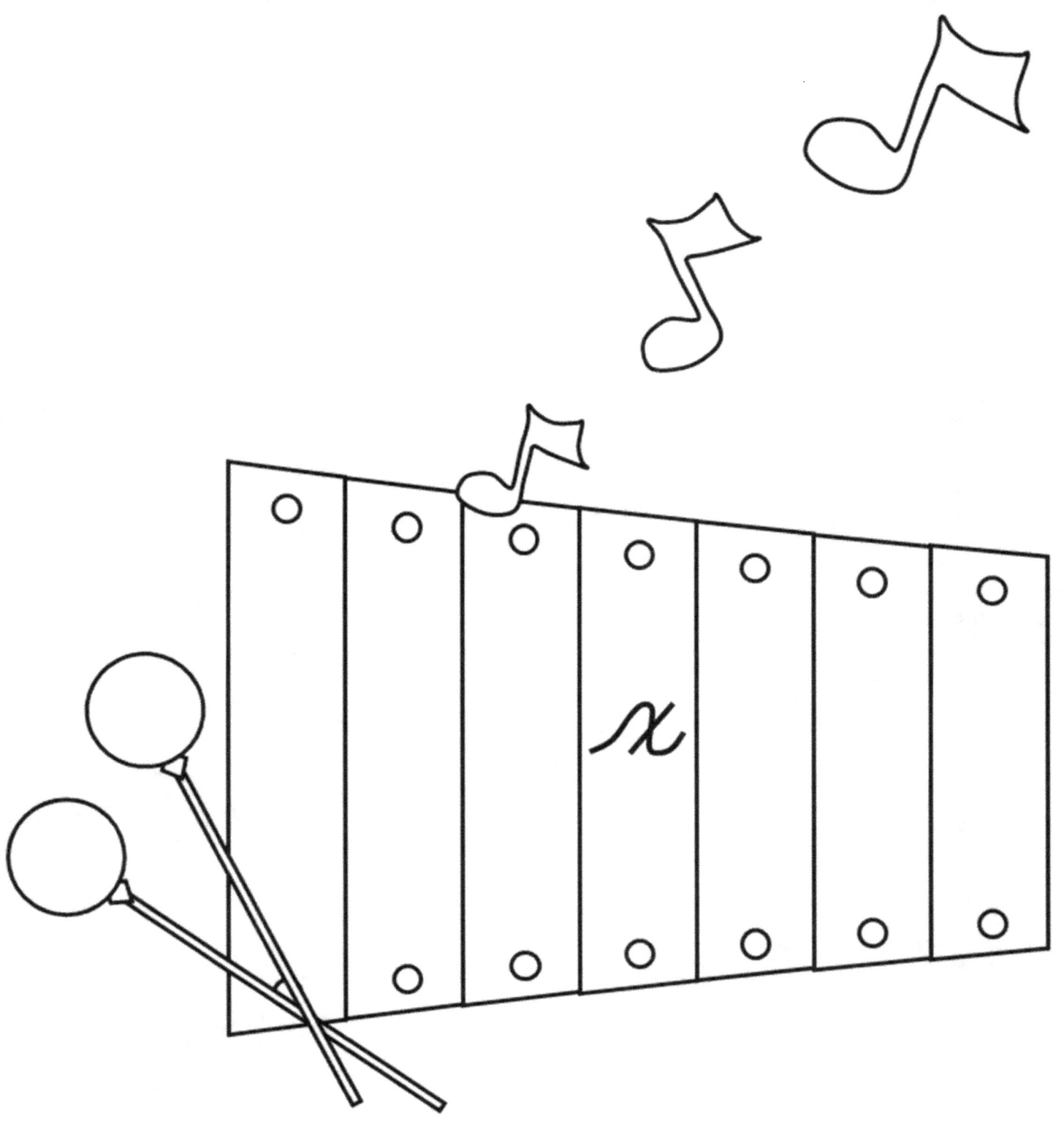

Trace the steps for making the letter x on the following line.

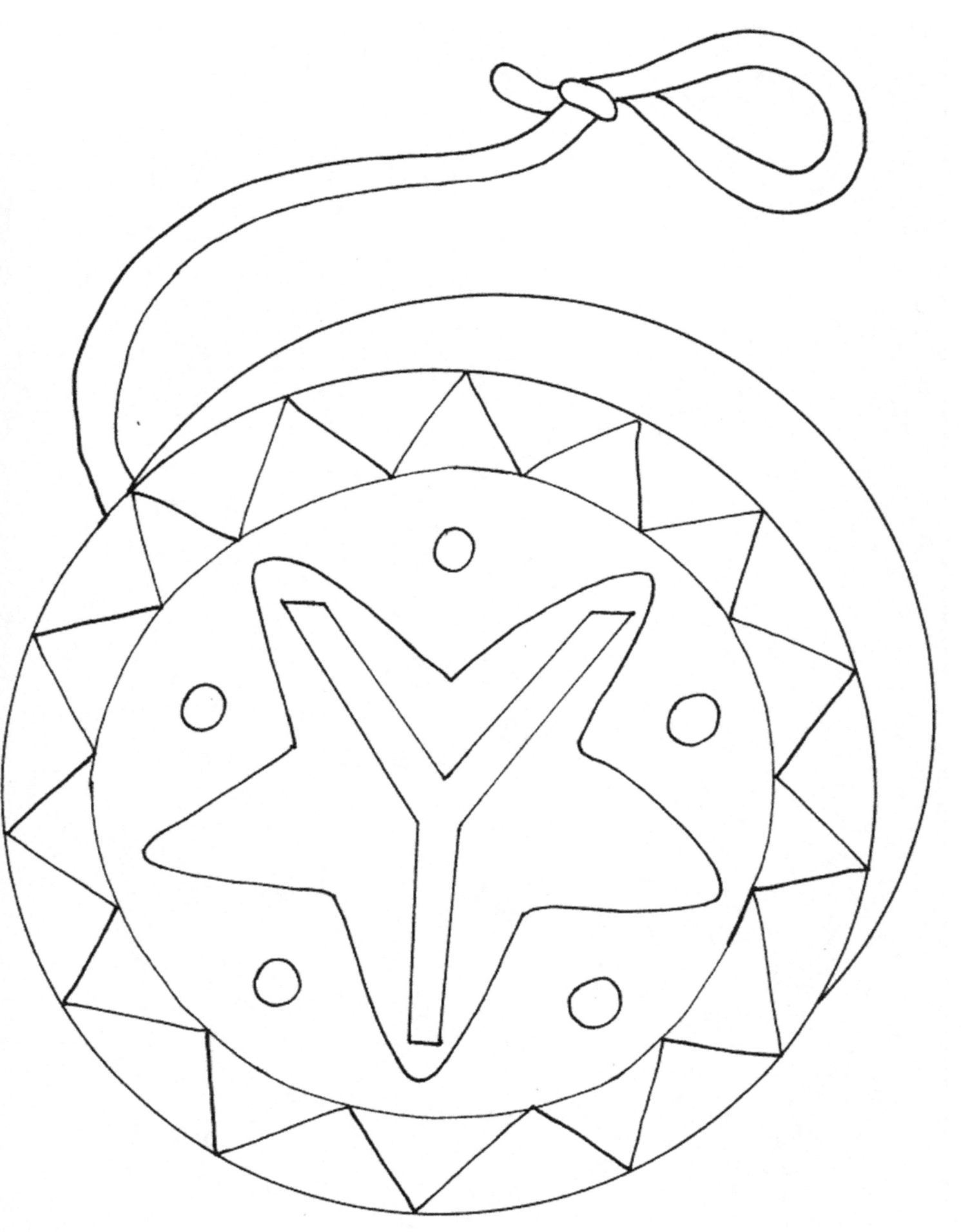

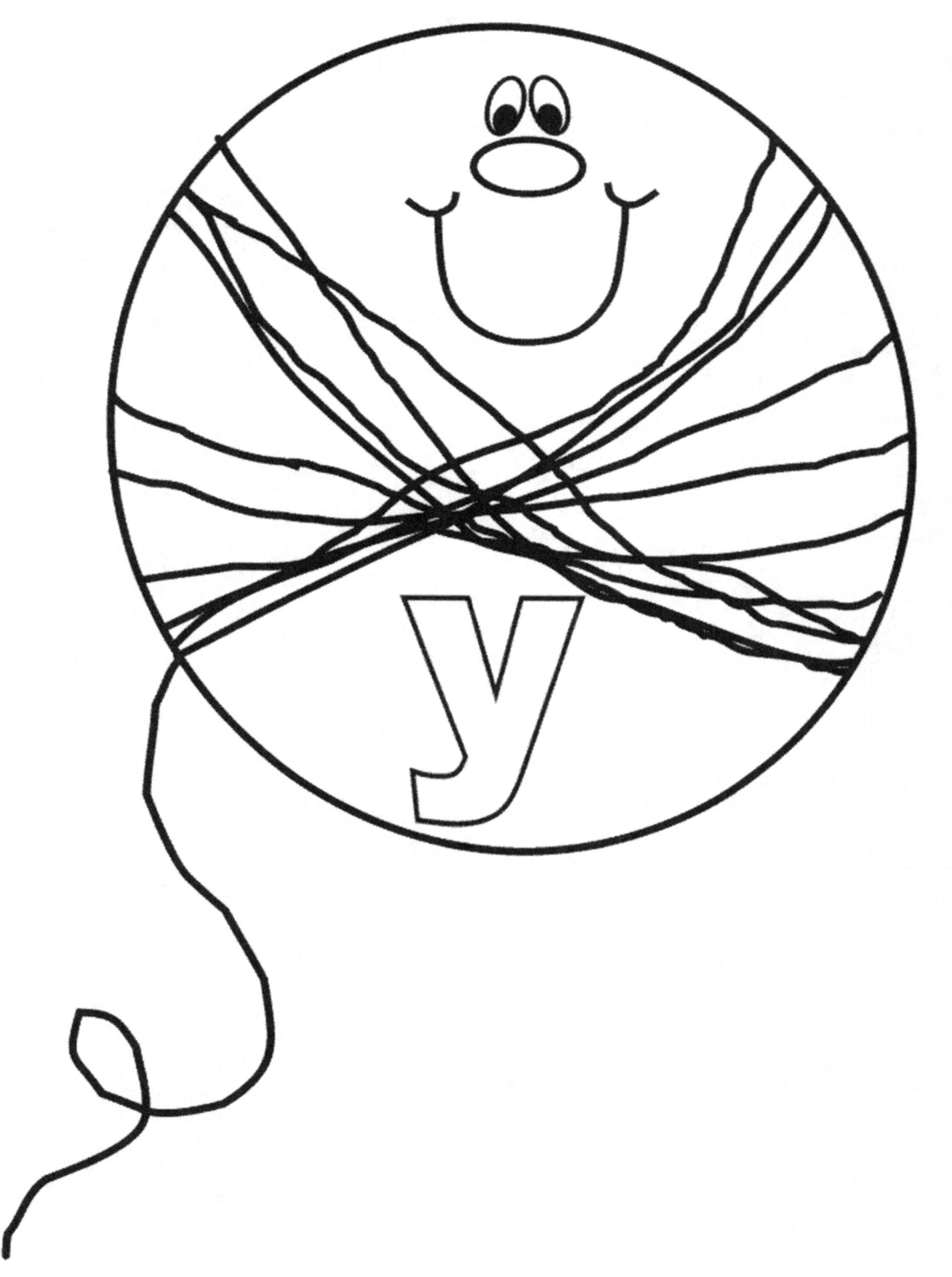

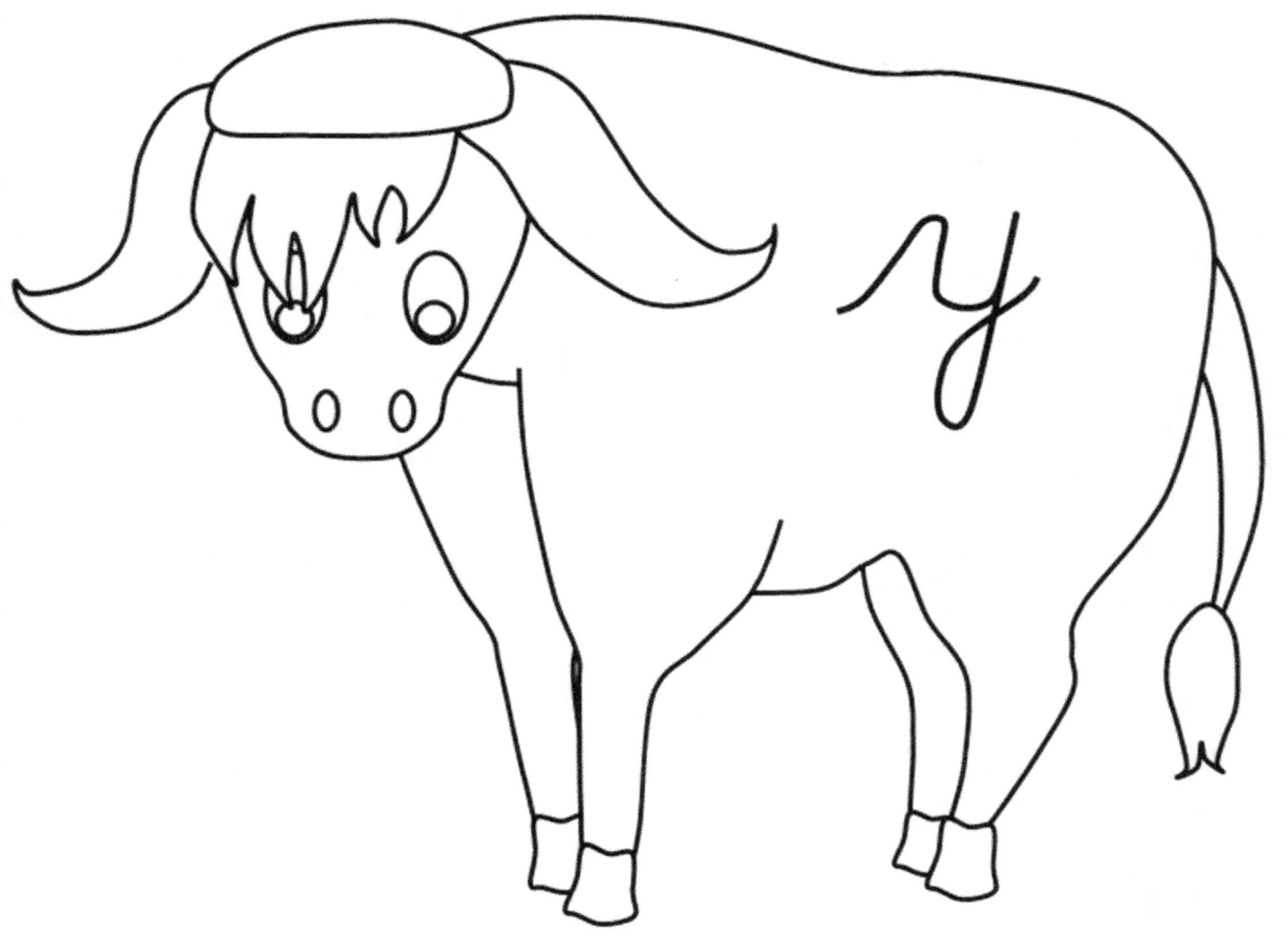

Trace the steps for making the letter y on the following line.

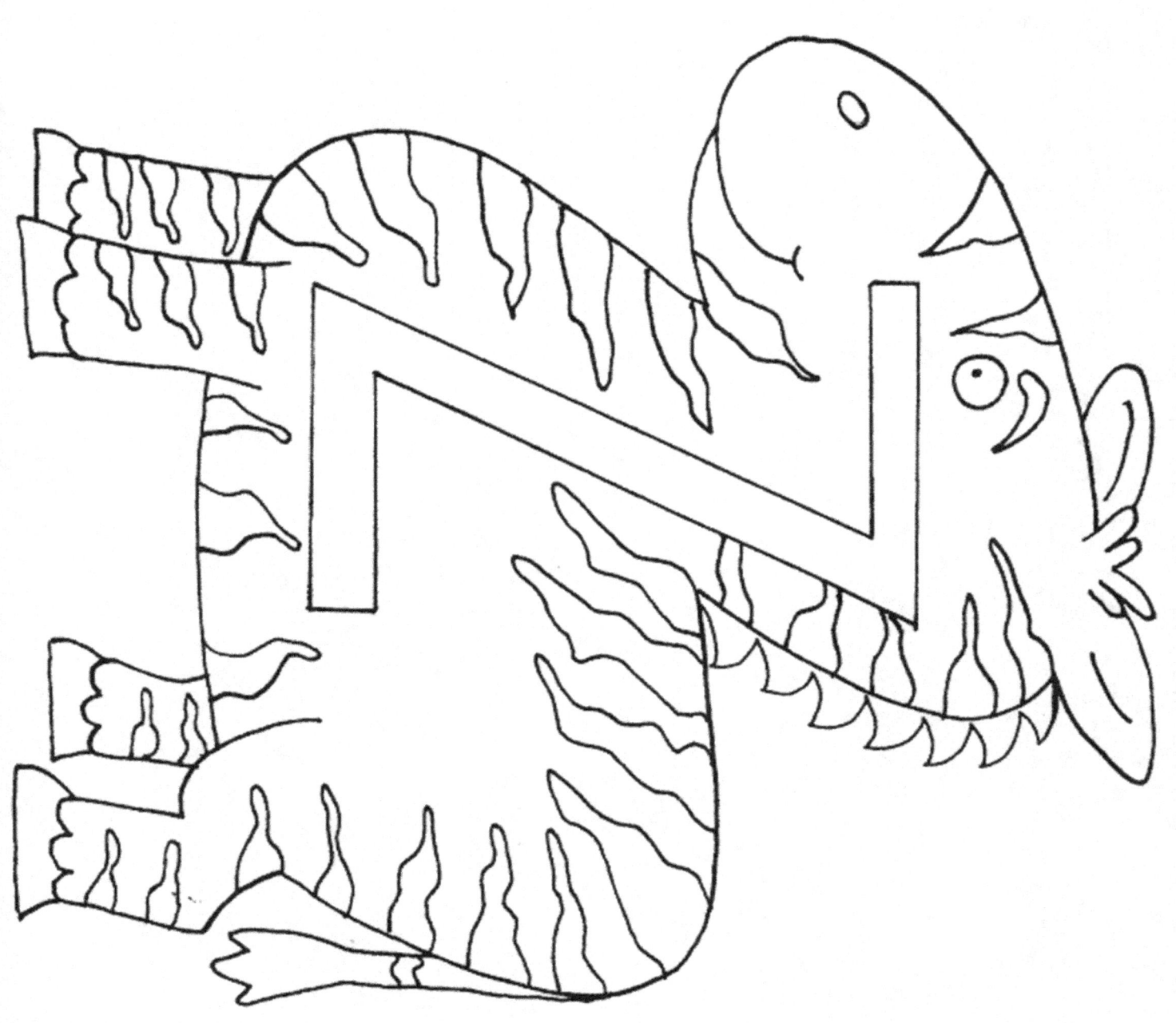

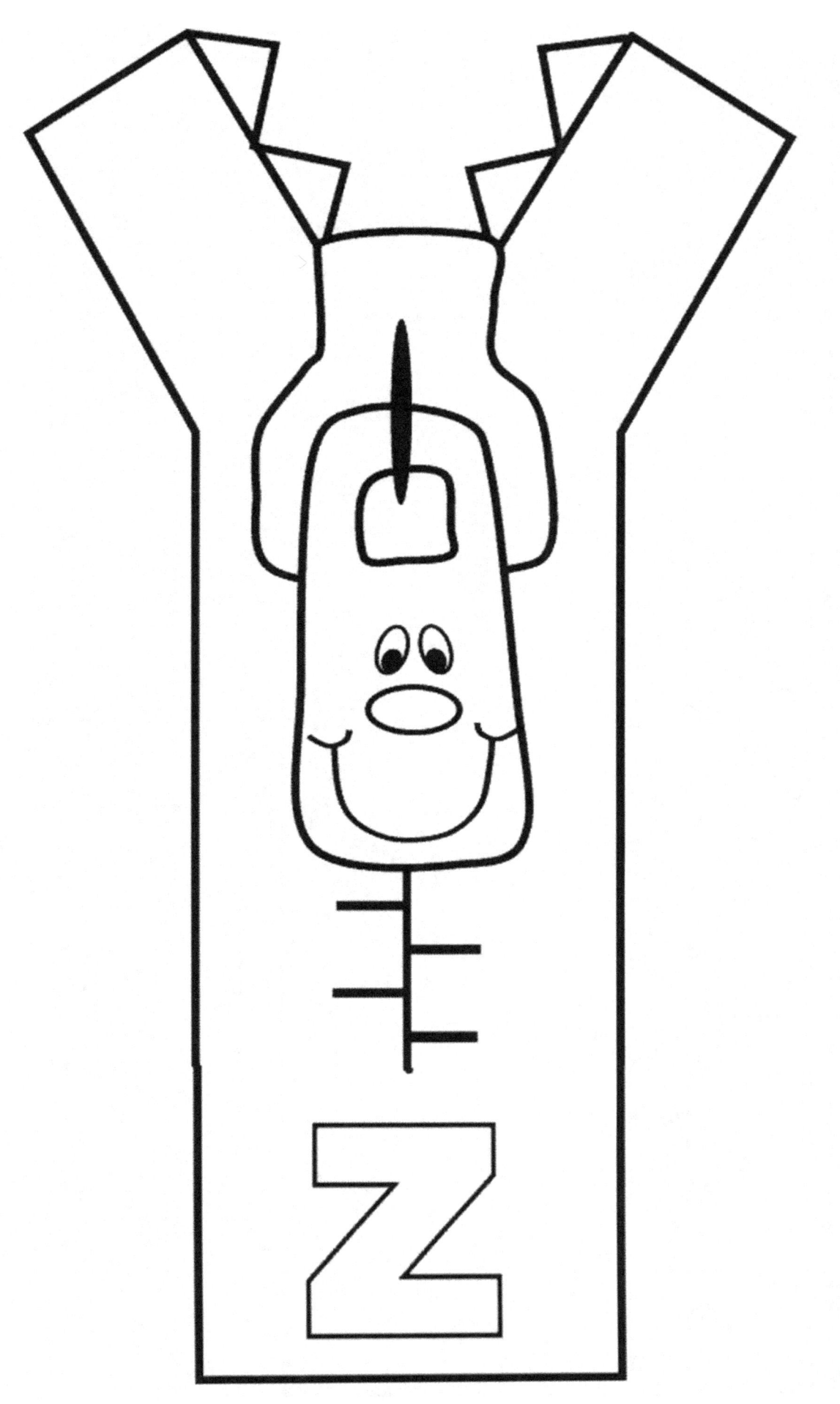

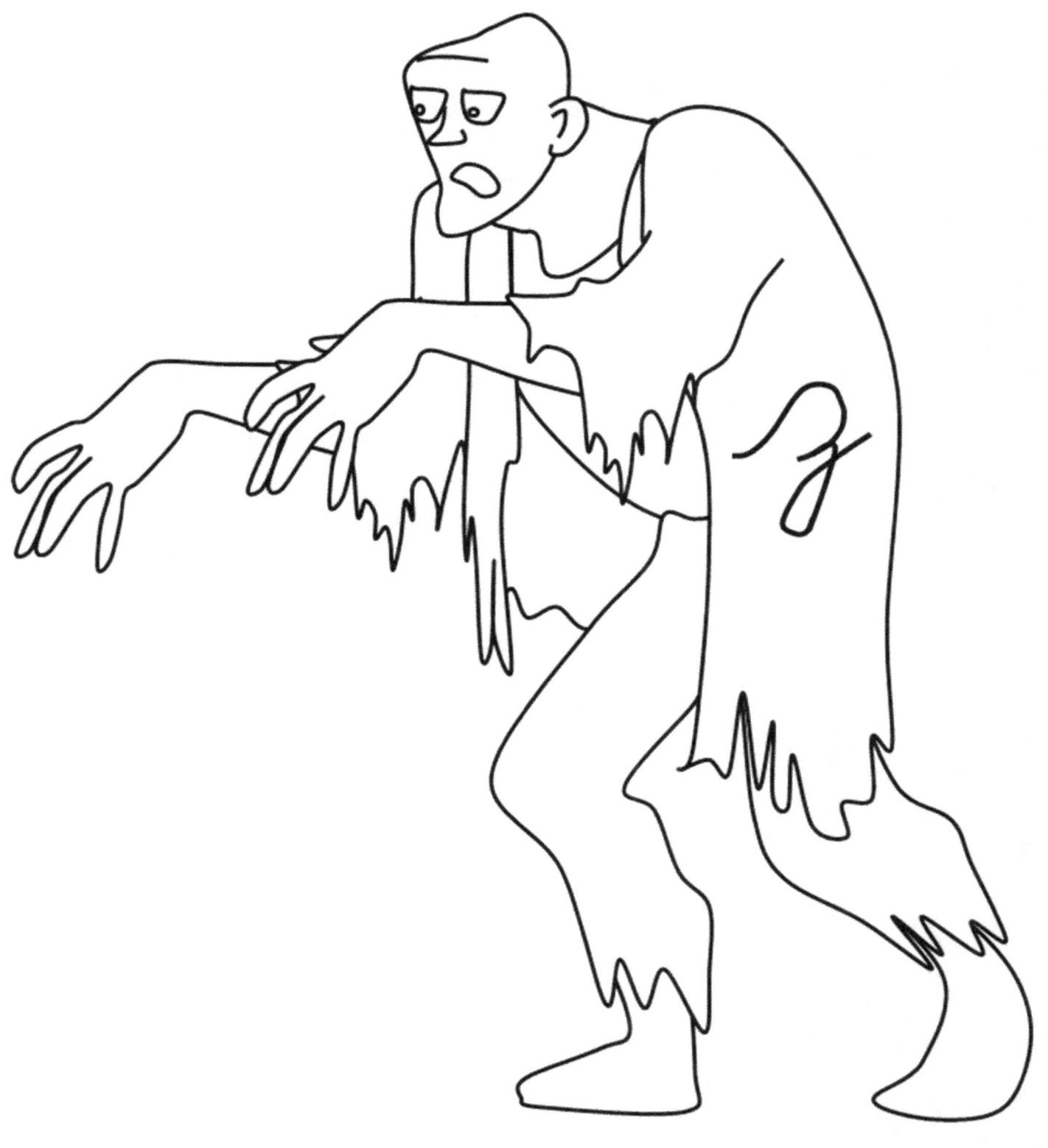

Trace the steps for making the letter z on the following line.